WALES
ON SCREEN

I would like to dedicate this book to my partner Mitch Winfield and to our two lovely children Sam and Beth

WALES
ON SCREEN

Edited by Steve Blandford

seren

seren is the book imprint of
Poetry Wales Press Ltd
Nolton Street, Bridgend, CF31 3BN, Wales
www.seren-books.com

ISBN 1-85411-248-1

A CIP record for this title is available from
the British Library

*The publisher works with the financial assistance of the
Arts Council of Wales*

Printed in Plantin by CPD Wales, Ebbw Vale

Contents

Foreword

I only discovered what the term 'film industry' meant when, while visiting Los Angeles for the first time, I opened the telephone book's Yellow Pages and discovered listing upon listing, page after page, sections and sections all devoted to the making and distributing of films.

The size and scale is quite difficult to comprehend because in 1998 the American film industry generated revenues of $6,949,000,000. The average cost of a film produced by a Hollywood studio was $52,700,000 – a cost which does not include monies spent on advertising which are often equal to the budget of a picture. The Motion Picture Association of America calculates that 541,700 people were employed by their industry last year.[1]

Given the size and scope of this, how can any other country's film-makers compete for screen-time, let alone an audience? How can a tiny country like Wales hope to make an impression?

In the 1970s 'new waves' of films from West Germany and Australia lit up cinemas. These films seemed to come from nowhere. There has been no groundswell or recent precursors, but within the space of a few years it appeared that both countries were knee-deep in talented film-makers both in front of and behind the camera.

Much was written at the time to explain the phenomena and the consensus conclusion was that German and Australian cultures were finally emerging from the detrimental influences of the Second World War, and UK culture, respectively.

With hindsight, however, it i very clear that while this was to some extent true, in both cases the suddenness of this increased film production was primarily because of economic changes created by the intervention of state and local governments, and television companies which *purposely* cultivated the conditions for filmmaking to flourish and compete with Hollywood – and one can only surmise that directors of the quality of Fassbinder, Herzog, Schlorndorff, Syberberg and Wenders; Armstrong,

Beresford, Miller, Schepsi, and Weir; and actors as accomplished as Bruno Ganz, Lisa Kreuzer, Bruni S., Hanna Schygulla, Rudliger Vogler; and Brian Brown, Judi Davies, Mel Gibson, and Sam Neill existed before 1970 in both countries, and has simply been unable to make or appear in films.

But what created the political will for this change? In the 'sixties neither country had a 'film culture' to speak of and there was certainly no international recognition of Australian or contemporary West German cinema. Within the space of a decade this had completely changed. While I have no idea what prompted the Australian government to restructure their tax laws to encourage investment in feature film production, I do know that in Germany the very filmmakers who were to emerge as 'auteurs' started a national debate which led to new approaches in the making and distribution of German films, of which they were the first beneficiaries.

Significantly for filmmakers in Britain, the success of Germany's ARD and ZDF television networks' investment in these new directors influenced the creation of Channel 4's 'Film Four' – which has arguably been the single biggest shot in the arm for British English-language filmmaking.

But between the emergence of the German New Wave and Channel 4's creation, European and American independent filmmakers – myself included – were making something of a pilgrimage to Köln, Berlin and Munich, hoping to get a piece of the German production monies which were rapidly disappearing even as we learnt of them.

I was shocked, on my first trip, to spend an evening in Dusseldorf listening to a table of dinner guests brutally disparage their 'New German Cinema'. They felt the films did not represent them, or anyone they knew and I found myself in the curious position of defending the New German Cinema to a group of vociferous and articulate Germans.

When I said that I believed *Aguirre, Wrath of God* to be close to a cinematic masterpiece, one of the dinner guests complained that it was old-fashioned and imperialistic, and followed the American model "because the Conquistadors speak German instead of Spanish or Portuguese." I felt rather foolish, because in all honesty I hadn't even noticed – and it didn't matter to me, just as it has never bothered me that Jimmy Caan – hardly an Italian-American – plays one of Don Corleone's sons in *The Godfather*, or that the Swedish Ingrid Bergman played an English missionary living in a China built in North Wales, or that the Polish-American Harvey Keitel can be a Maori. That, to me has always been part and parcel of the suspension of disbelief one enters into when going to see a larger-than-life world in a darkened room illuminated by a succession of flickering photographs.

I left the Dusseldorf dinner party puzzled, but in one of life's rather wonderful ironies, I was to find myself in America, in the late 'eighties, at a friend's home, holding forth on what all *I* thought was wrong about Channel 4's Film Four productions – while my American friends, for whom Film Four's output was exotic, defended them.

At that time a curious disparity had arisen, because while British films were being successfully screened in the United States, they were failing to find cinema audiences in the UK. Indeed, the big leap in UK production – and the confidence which funded it – can be traced to the moment when canny US distributors, realising that here was a classy product they could buy cheap and sell dear – stepped in and gave British films access to the largest English speaking audience, reminding me of the John Landis line about his success and the way in which "producers lined up to give me the opportunity to make more money for them."

Like the Germans at the dinner table in Dusseldorf, I, the exiled Welshman in LA, said that Film Four's output was unrepresentative. I – especially as an Anglo-Welshman – felt excluded and invisible.

"Who, for you," asked an American woman, "is a quintessential American director?" I answered, "Martin Scorsese", because I couldn't see his mix of subject matter, confident bravura, naturalistic acting, fractured narrative and fast-paced cutting coming from anywhere but American cinema. The woman agreed with me but then pointed out that she was a Protestant from the dairy farms of Wisconsin. "You really think Marty represents *me*?" she asked, continuing, "You think those films have any relationship to the realities of *my* life?"

These thought about national and international cinema, who or what conditions create it, who we hope will watch it and who actually watches it, who feels represented and who doesn't, inevitably came to mind while reading *Wales on Screen.*

The writers represent a diverse group who, taken together, give a comprehensive, multi-dimensional snapshot of a moment when, it seems, Wales may have a good chance of creating, and sustaining a cinema and television culture which will have relevance both in and outside its borders. Such cinema and television will only come from debate – and in itself will be a debate – a debate to which, I'm pleased to say, this book actively contributes.

Christopher Monger, May 1999, Los Angeles.

[1] Taken from the MPAA website: www.mpaa.org

Introduction

During the time it has taken to conceive and compile this volume there have been moments when it has genuinely seemed that Wales' contribution to the development of contemporary film and television drama was being recognised and even fêted by the mainstream media. Admittedly a lot of the coverage was still vaguely patronising, but it also grudgingly acknowledged that something new was emerging in Wales, namely a film culture that was attempting to shake off the dead hand of old debates about national identity and marginalisation. Instead we were seeing at least the beginnings of an 'industry' that saw its identity in much more open and fluid terms; in relation to European cinemas, in relation to the success of Welsh independent rock music and in relation to the success of the other Celtic film industries to name but three.

This is of course to start with the good news and it is part of what this book is about to try to cut through some of the hype and examine the real state of the Welsh film and television industries. To date the solid achievements of the emerging talents in film remain relatively small. *Twin Town* ruffled feathers at home and did better at the box office than any previous 'Welsh' film, though its critical reception was mixed. *House of America* had more art house leanings and did better critically without quite achieving quite the impact (outside Wales) that it hoped for.

Most recently Justin Kerrigan's *Human Traffic* has had arguably the best mixture of box office success and positive critical reception of any Welsh film, certainly of the last twenty years, Sara Sugarman is about to convert a string of short film plaudits into a feature career with the release of *Mad Cows*, whilst as the book goes to press, arguably the highest profile film to date with strong Welsh credentials, *Rancid Aluminium* is released, marking the feature directorial debut of Ed Thomas.

Wales-based initiatives in the comparatively neglected areas of short fiction and animation have also been significant. The siting of the International Animation Festival in Cardiff has a lot to say about the country's recent record of producing both successful commercial products and innovative individual talents (including the 1998 Oscar-nominee Joanna Quinn). In 'Short Fiction', a joint venture by BBC Wales and the then Welsh Film Council produced a series of critically acclaimed short films under the umbrella title of PICS and another 1998 one-off short *The Deadness of Dad* was acclaimed widely enough to not only be shown on the network by the BBC but repeated.

In television the jury is decidedly still out as Dave Berry's piece in this volume implies. The distinguishing feature of BBC Wales drama department over the last decade has arguably been constant change; of actual personnel and linked inextricably to this of policy direction. When this project was conceived Karl Francis was about to begin his improbable stint as head of that department, one year later he was gone and Pedr James and an enlarged team are attempting to build a solid indigenous writer base. With the latest changes to the BBC's own internal funding structure there is also a likelihood of slightly more money for the 'right product': there is now a commitment by London to commission at least a third of its drama output from the regions. In the commercial sector too there is the welcome recent news of HTV's plans to double its annual drama production from the admittedly very low base of ten hours. The latter too has a new drama team with a commitment to re-invigorate an area that has come in for so much criticism over the last decade. The broadcast of the Merthyr-based *Nuts and Bolts* will be an important test here.

To these new shoots we might add the formation of a new 'media agency' for Wales in Sgrîn, based in Cardiff Bay, which will hope to emulate its Scottish equivalent in nurturing new talent, though in the current situation this will be inextricably linked to what the lottery can provide.

Finally, since 1998 Cardiff has hosted two international film festivals. As stated above, it has been home to the International Animation Festival for some years now, but it was recently announced that the burgeoning Wales International Film Festival is to move from its original base in Aberystwyth to Cardiff, a politically loaded decision indeed for some people, but one defended on the grounds that the festival's primary reason for existence is to promote Wales and the film-makers of Wales, and the only criteria for locating it should be the best place from which to do that.

In a nutshell these are the most prominent features of the current situation, some of which are well developed in the subsequent essays in this volume. Perhaps though it is pertinent here to reflect for a moment on what a Welsh film and television industry with a significant output specifically in *fiction* (because this is the principal concern of this volume) might mean if it can be said to exist at all and even more fundamentally what it might be *for*.

A straight comparison with Scotland for instance has always been problematic because of the existence of S4C. This is not to be so perverse as to argue that the existence of a channel whose primary aim is to promote the Welsh language is a disadvantage *per se*. It is rather that the implicit assumptions made by policy makers both inside and outside the industry as a result of S4C's existence have resulted in a significant diminution of opportunities for film-makers in the English language in Wales. Karl Francis' threat in 1993 to take Channel 4 to the race relations board for discriminating against Welsh-originated material was really just a more robust response to a widely perceived problem: Wales had S4C and not only Channel 4 but implicitly the BBC in London and the ITV Network Centre could cheerfully ignore all things Welsh because Wales had its own (very expensive) channel. As John Hill wrote in a recent useful study of the growth of film and TV's interdependency in this country:

> In the case of Wales, the significance of Channel Four has been the establishment of its Welsh-language television service, S4C.[1]

During the last two decades when the relationship between film and television in the UK has become so inextricably linked this has proved a powerful disadvantage not only to Wales' profile on small screens, but also to its emergence as a small-scale film making culture. It was a period in which, as Andrew Higson and others have pointed out, Channel 4 not merely 'saved' the British film industry but became its virtual 'life-support machine.'[2] Welsh talent, particularly those working in

English, had its machine turned off.

This goes further than the bald fact of very few commissions going to Welsh writers, directors and producers. As John Hill suggests, Channel Four have not been in feature production to make profits. For every *Four Weddings and a Funeral* there are a dozen risky box office flops:

> ...it has to an extent 'subsidised' film production insofar as the relatively high percentage of the Channel's overall budget (6.2 per cent between 1982 and 1992) devoted to Film on Four has not been matched by the number of programme hours or audience ratings which it has provided. As Isaacs [Jeremy, Channel 4's first chief executive] explained in the early days of Film on Four, he regarded such films as having a 'socio-cultural provenance and purpose' which went beyond their financial returns or contributions to the ratings.[3]

What this has meant for Wales is that in a formative period for the modern British film industry it has lacked access to a source of funding specifically designed to encourage risk-taking, the tackling of sensitive or unpopular subjects and the work of young or lesser known film-makers. Even if one accepts that the innovatory nature of Film on Four has been overstated, its achievements alongside those of Channel 4's Department of Independent Film and Video are substantial enough to make the almost total absence of Welsh projects very significant indeed.

Lest it be thought that S4C has made no contribution at all, it is important to draw attention to both Dave Berry and Tim Robbins and Chris Webster's surveys later in the book and to single out the channel's nurturing of feature-film talents such as Endaf Emlyn, Paul Turner and more recently Ceri Sherlock. But there are huge differences here. One of the most uncomfortable statistics in Wales is that S4C's Welsh language output serves only around 600,000 people out of a total population of around 3 million, but more significantly still, the channel never had Channel Four's remit to encourage innovation. With honourable exceptions, some of which I have already mentioned, this has meant an output in fiction which has reflected the generally traditional nature of its core audience. This may change: the language is now growing much faster than it had in the south and amongst the young; we have seen responses to this from parts of the burgeoning music industry and it is possible that film may eventually follow. Work such as Endaf Emlyn's *Gadael Lenin,* and for the small screen, the Ceri Sherlock directed *Dafydd,* suggest that the beginnings are already there.

This all returns us rather to the question of what a Welsh film and TV fiction industry might be for. At one level the answer is obvious; all cultures that want to survive need to represent themselves to the wider world and to themselves. More specifically in this context though, there is an urgent need to build up a 'critical mass' of representations that will in themselves relieve writers and film-makers generally from a particular sort of burden. In the early 1980's John Caughie, writing in a volume with similar aims to this one except in relation to Scotland, said:

> It is simply that there is a limited amount of institutional and financial support for the production of Scottish discourses, with the result that there is a highly restricted range of images available for the presentation of Scottishness. Whereas the representations of English country life in *All Creatures Great and Small* take their place within a range of other images from situation comedies, police series, single plays (etc.), the representations of *Dr Finlay's Casebook* or *Take The High Road* became the consistent and recurrent images of Scottishness available at the time.[4]

Since this was written of course, the range of representations of Scotland in circulation has increased enormously and embraces not just *Tutti Frutti* and *Taggart* but also *Shallow Grave* and *Trainspotting.* The result of this for the likes of *Hamish Macbeth* is that they are free of a particularly irksome kind of burden, the sort which *Tiger Bay* almost certainly laboured very heavily under.

Ed Thomas and Marc Evans talk persuasively later in this volume about their desire to be rid of a lot of the older sterile debates about Welsh identity, particularly those with the greatest tendency to polarise contributors, and it is surely a confident contemporary film and television industry that is best placed to make this happen. In another interview Thomas makes an attempt to almost quantify the 'critical mass' that might at least redefine the terms of the debate:

If in the next ten years Wales were to produce three major novels, five acclaimed English-language films, six plays and superb work by two visual artists and if all these became known throughout Britain and Europe, then you could really say that the total of all these things would have invented a new Welsh culture.[5]

I would add to this a significant presence in drama on network television, but there are many, including Thomas, who understandably have given up on that.

So in Wales we might say that film and television fictions are part of a process not simply of redefining stale stereotypes, but of ridding people of the burden of worrying about them at all. This though still leaves us with the (often sterile) debates about what such a proliferation of discourses might have to say about the culture.

In a recent essay about the issues surrounding theatre in Wales, David Adams talks interestingly about the 'orientalisation' of Wales, its 'invention' as a kind of exotic other entity by the neighbouring colonial power in a way analogous to the invention of India, China or Japan. This in its turn, he argues, has met the virtually global appropriation of popular culture by all things American so that to search for an authentic contemporary Welsh voice is to say the least, highly problematic:

No wonder cultural confusion reigns. On the one hand contemporary Wales can be seen as an ideological construct, a product of political discourse, an 'Other' invented by a neighbouring oppressor, translated into and assumed as a set of stereotypes, often expressed in purely racist terms; on the other, absorbed by England and America into an amorphous identity, invisible even, echoing still that notorious 1910 *Encyclopaedia Britannica* entry "For Wales, see England."[6]

What cinema and television has the capacity to do is transform the old debates much more rapidly and within discourses that can most readily reach out and fire the imaginations of the young in geographical areas not traditionally blessed by the visitations of the Welsh cultural establishment. Until the recent *Human Traffic*, its attempts to do this were united only by a loosely post-modern engagement with the very debates and stereotypes from which it wants to be free, as even a brief examination of the three films involved in the much trumpeted

Welsh film 'boom' year will show.

Twin Town, House of America and the less well-known *Darklands* were all released within months of each other in 1997 and all, in very different ways, present to the world a Wales that is as far from male voice choirs and rugby as *Shallow Grave* and *Trainspotting* were from the 'Tartanry and Kailyard'[7] of the once dominant filmic representations of Scotland. Yet all (like *Trainspotting* to a limited extent – I refer to the speech were Ewan MacGregor sits on a heathery hill-top and berates his fellow countrymen for their endless obsession with defining themselves in relation to the English) contain implicit or explicit engagement with the 'orientalised' vision of Welshness that they seek to cast off.

Twin Town, the nearest of the three to making an impact on a wider UK popular culture landscape, does this in the most irreverent way to the extent that it brought down the almost inevitable (but still hugely comic) wrath of the tourist board and Swansea civic authorities. Daryl Perrins' piece in this volume effectively re-reads *Twin Town* and rescues it from the idea that it is damaging to Wales on any level, so here we will look at Kevin Allen's film very briefly.

Perhaps *Twin Town*'s biggest handicap stems from what undoubtedly got it made in the first place; its connections with the *Trainspotting* team of Andrew Macdonald and Danny Boyle as producers. This resulted in a large number of unfavourable comparisons in the national press and even condemnation from *Sight and Sound,* whose reviewer opens with snide sideswipes at what he calls the picture's "eagerness to be to South Wales what *Trainspotting* was to urban Scotland" and goes on to an extremely odd piece of moralising from a magazine of this nature:

> It seems to take pleasure in its leading characters' lack of any redeeming features, and from the dog's decapitation through the death of the twins' whole family to the concluding clutch of 'comic' murders (in themselves enough to drive the most diehard defender of free speech kicking and screaming into the censorship lobby) a streak of sadism as wide as the M4 runs through the entire narrative.[8]

Those concerned with tourism and the image of the City of Swansea had more specific, material concerns than the high-minded Mr Thompson (above) of course. They were worried that all the efforts to attract people to a Wales that they had worked so hard to construct (as a land of sheep, choirs and Celtic twilight) were being undermined and would have preferred Mel Gibson as Owain Glyndwr no doubt.

Perhaps *Twin Town* was a little stuck in the wake of *Trainspotting* and it is undoubtedly not overly-concerned with new Welsh filmic discourses! But that is in a sense the point; it has this elusive confidence, alluded to by several of the contributors to this volume, to either ignore the obvious ways to 'be Welsh' or to laugh at them from within. Its reported reception with Welsh audiences suggests that for younger people at least it is a confidence that is beginning to be shared. However, as Nigel Morris recently pointed out, the reaction of sections of the Welsh intellectual establishment suggests the need for quite a substantial quantity of irreverence yet:

> The film itself was attacked by clergy – whose warnings of copycat poodle beheadings surpassed the satire on screen – perpetuating a century of mistrust epitomised by the poem 'Beware of the Cinema' by Reverend Thomas David Evans.[9]

Julian Richards' debut feature *Darklands* is the nearest of the three to a genre piece, but ironically therefore the one to have received least widespread distribution. Its treatment of traditional Welsh icons is potentially the most subversive and irreverent of the three, though as Dave Berry has said, the tone of the piece should make us wary of drawing too many strong political conclusions.[10]

Drawing heavily and openly on Robin Hardy's cult British horror piece *The Wicker Man* (1973), Richards' film attempts the very difficult job of combining the devastated industrial landscapes of South Wales (the crucial scenes shot on location in Port Talbot) with a particular take on paganism, druids and a brand of Welsh Nationalism that is seen to be openly linked to fascist ideas. The central character is a journalist investigating a number of instances of animal sacrifices which lead him to suspect a local nationalist businessman. This then develops nto a sometimes fascinating but also improbable plot involving forced impregnation, human sacrifice and the linking of ancient fertility rituals with attempts at modern urban renewal. The villain is of course the neo-Nazi nationalist businessman.

As Dave Berry suggests, Richards has certainly associated himself in the past with those lamenting the lack of opportunities for monoglot English speakers in the Welsh film and television industries, and although perhaps a little tongue in cheek, in his first feature he has been brave enough to take risks while working within an always prickly local political culture.

> My film's not primarily political [Richards says now]. But the Devolution vote proved that Wales remains a deeply divided country and part of my agenda was to say that, in Wales, English language culture has a right to exist equally.[11]

Perhaps not surprisingly, neither *Darklands* nor the third of the trilogy under consideration – *House of America,* fared much better at the hands of the UK critical establishment than did *Twin Town.* In the context of this discussion it was particularly interesting to see *Sight and Sound* criticise Richards for his attacks on a particular kind of Welsh identity, when from the safe distance of London the Welsh industry is virtually always ignored altogether:

> ...*Darklands* remains boringly on the side of the (English-speaking) status quo, offering little insight into Celtic, pagan or even Welsh nationalist beliefs, let alone inviting us to flirt with sharing them.[12]

House of America, whilst probably faring the best of the three in terms of overall critical reception, still incurred the wrath of the *Sight and Sound* reviewer assigned to it. '*House*' is treated extensively elsewhere in this volume, but what seems to link its review with those of the other two films is a kind of displeasure at the ways Welsh film has taken on its own heritage and tried to develop an ironic discourse around it. *House of America* it seems to me was criticised mostly for avoiding too scrupulously the observance of the "small commonplace things" (*Sight and Sound,* see below) so beloved of the mainstream British film tradition and instead substituting a range of linguistic and visual pyrotechnics. This in turn made it hard for reviewers to see it as a credible film "detailing the frustrations of being stranded in a one-street town in South Wales with no jobs, no money and no hope."[13] In other words it was being criticised for failing to be, as Ed Thomas puts in the later interview, a British miserabilist film; something in fact that it set out scrupulously to avoid.

During the next decade it will be interesting to see whether a film culture develops with the confidence to make films without even the ironic reference to traditional Welsh iconography that this latest wave has made. Meanwhile it is surely not insignificant that the core of English critical opinion generally seems to misunderstand and dislike Welsh attempts to not so much avoid the stereotypes, but deconstruct them from within.

★ ★ ★

The essays in this volume are not themed in any sense except a desire to shed light on the current state of the Welsh film and television industries with a particular emphasis on drama. The book was conceived partly as a response to the fact that similar collections were available on Scotland, to which I have already referred, and Ireland, but not Wales.[14] Of course any work on these industries in Wales has to acknowledge a huge debt to Dave Berry's tremendously useful and important historical work, but this much less ambitious book is about something else;[15] that is to assess the two inextricably linked industries at what many have seen as a vital moment in their development and to look to how the immediate future might build upon a promising current situation.

Another loose governing principle was to bring together in one volume two categories of contributors that are so often wastefully suspicious of each other; namely 'industry professionals' and academics. Of course, some of the writers straddle both camps and others don't fit very easily into either, but the aim remained to bridge something of a divide and to therefore provide a mix of viewpoints that might open up the kinds of debates and dialogue that are the whole point of this type of work.

Michelle Ryan's contribution comes from a position which not only bridges the divide mentioned above (she has now worked for a number of years as a full-time director, but was also at one time a full-time lecturer in Communication Studies at the old Polytechnic of Wales, and acts as a visiting lecturer on a number of film and television courses) but also, as much as anyone, has been at the heart of so many aspects of the current scene in Wales. She can talk first hand of working with the mainstream television channels, of the heady days of the workshop sector, and of the new, highly competitive Welsh independent production scene, through her long association with probably the best known independent of them all, Teliesyn.

Her piece is not particularly optimistic; not about the Welsh industry, but about its inability to find a much needed source of energy and inspiration for specifically female voices. In certain respects perhaps her account is of women going backwards in the Welsh industry from a high point where Red Flannel and others were producing some of the most innovative material to come out of the UK workshop sector. With the virtual demise of these kinds of spaces meeting a cultural backlash calling itself post-feminism head-on it could be argued that 'a woman's place' in Wales has got gradually smaller. With its particularly strong patriarchal, cultural and political traditions, Wales, it seems, is particularly vulnerable to a more widespread phenomenon.

As a valuable corrective to this, though, Michelle Ryan does also point to a significant body of younger women film-makers that is now emerging. What tends to unite them she argues is a concentration on the cinema as opposed to television where the unspoken male rules of large-scale hierarchies are less of a factor.

One of those she mentions, Cardiff animator Joanna Quinn is now relatively established and earlier this year received the valuable publicity of an Oscar nomination. Sara Sugarman too is currently working on two high-profile feature projects having turned out a number of impressive short films, including *Valley Girls,* which took the D.M. Davies Award at the 1997 Welsh International Film Festival. Like Sugarman, both Margaret Constantas and Phillipa Cousins have announced themselves with impressive shorts that have taken awards at BAFTA Cymru and the Celtic Film Festival respectively.

Perhaps, as Michelle Ryan urges, these women will emerge as role models that may finally lead to a more developed and sustained presence for women in film and television in Wales; what is already evident is that women have been very prominent in taking advantage of the opportunities offered by short film initiatives in Wales such as PICS, even if they have been longer coming than parallel schemes such as Scotland's *Tartan Shorts*.

Philip John's highly personal account of someone trying to work and be true to their own cinematic vision is suitably both sobering and occasionally inspiring. In his introductory first half he makes comparisons with Scotland as do others in this volume, reaches the conclusion that so much can be down to individuals and a will to make a film and television culture succeed. Certainly BBC Scotland's record, first under Bill Bryden and then Andrea Calderwood has, as Phil John says "laid the foundations for a generation of bold, culturally assertive Scottish film-makers," something that could most certainly not be said about the drama department in Cardiff over the same period. However as the rest of John's essay bears testimony to, it clearly goes beyond individual visionaries, crucial as they are. Andrea Calderwood, Head of Drama at BBC Scotland at the time reflected in 1996 on a highly success-ful previous year for Scottish film drama and some of what she has to say is full of bitter irony for people in the same position which Phil John so entertainingly describes:

> The majority of the Scottish producers who had their scripts backed by SFPF [Scottish Film Production Fund] and got their films made in this last year had little or no track record in producing feature films. It was only the ability to finance properly the development of their projects to the stage where the strength of the script could allow them to create a viable production package, or convince sources of production finance of the viability of the film, that put their projects in a position to make the leap from being nice ideas to being films that got made.[16]

Calderwood goes on to specify the difference made not only by the SFPF's substantial and bold support, but also that of the Glasgow Film Fund. A grim comparison again with John's account of his experiences at the Wales Film Council and BBC Wales.

To set against this 'The Story of A Welsh Screenplay' does also offer hope almost in spite of itself, particularly the section that is an edited version of Phil John's 'Work Journal' over a six year period from 1992-8. It is a vivid account of somebody with powerful roots in a part of Wales that has been not only economically devastated from without, but neglected by its own cultural establishment, having the confidence and sheer guts to look to Europe for sources of funding, to relish the chance to take part in often bruising encounters with readers of his script, to pay "the price of a small car for two coffees and a juice" at Cannes in order to hawk the script yet again and to look to the likes of Canadian Atom Egoyan for inspiration. In short, it is the tale of somebody who works in Wales and is cine-literate and streetwise in a European sense and I'm sure Phil John would be the first to admit that he is not alone. The message is clearly that this deserves a more vigorous leg-up from a re-emerging culture that aspires to the status of young imaginative nationhood.

Tim Robbins and Chris Webster's 'Between Nation and Animation, the Fear of a Mickey Mouse Planet', not only provides a useful and comprehensive survey of the important animation industry developed in Wales over the last twenty years, but also reminds us of the unique role animated fictions play in the formation (and destruction) of national identities across the planet. Apart perhaps from McDonalds and Coca-Cola, the products of Disney studios have become for many the most visible symbol of American cultural and economic hegemony. Worse still, at least two of the three frequently combine forces so that the characters your children make you watch a thousand times on video also pop terrifyingly, in miniature, out of the styro-foam packaging the next time you are press-ganged into lunch with Ronald.

Whilst not neglecting the threat of American cultural products, Robbins and Webster interestingly challenge the knee-jerk thesis of universal condemnation of all things Disney in favour of those of a 'local' industry. They argue persuasively that for all S4C's fostering of an industry, from early attempts to 'take on' Disney and Time Warner to today's tendency towards 'niche-marketing' that production policy in Wales is always caught in between a vaguely expressed desire to make a contribution to concern over "our own indigenous culture being eroded by Anglicisation" and the need to sell in international markets. As Robbins and Webster point out, it is not widely known just how expensive animation is; they quote two million pounds for an animated series of 13x10 minute episodes of a major children's TV series. The resulting imperatives for international marketability are obvious, and one of the most prominent of recent S4C-backed animation projects, *Animation Classics*, far from projecting anything like a Welsh identity is much more to do with "particular constructions of Britishness," as Robbins and Webster put it.

Finally though, as the authors recognise, it is not a simple matter of trying to retreat into a siege position (even if that were viable) in the face of transnational challenge. They do not offer solutions, but rather urge upon the media industries in general and the animation industry in Wales in particular, a recognition of complexity:

> If the people of Wales are to be assembled and are to see themselves and each other as Welsh and to hold each other in mutual regard then what will be needed from the media industries and its products are complex ways of seeing. Simple oppositions will not do.

Many would argue that the creation of not only a burgeoning animation sector, but an animation culture (recognised by the siting of the International Festival here) is one of the most tangible achievements in the pursuit of a genuine Welsh film and television industry. Tim Robbins and Chris Webster give this due recognition whilst raising complex questions about its relationship to a wider international picture and in turn about the viability of a small film and television industry's contribution to national identity in the context of a global market place.

The interview with Ed Thomas and Marc Evans draws attention not only to the film that has borne the biggest burden of critical expectation as the vanguard of a new young Welsh cinema, but also to two of the individuals that have been most often seen as carrying the hopes of an indigenous film industry. Ed Thomas in particular, perhaps against his will, has often been seen as something much wider still; the new voice of not only Welsh cinema but also theatre and popular television and during the 1997 referendum campaign – he seemed to be asked his views as almost as much as any politician. Evans, meanwhile, has begun to build an international reputation as a director following a series of television and short film successes.

It is perhaps ironic then that it is they, and Thomas in particular, who are amongst the most sceptical of this volume's contributors in relation to there being a burgeoning Welsh industry at all. With good humour Ed Thomas continually refers here, and in numerous interviews, to a 'despite culture' in Wales: *House of America*, his own Fiction Factory now grown into a flourishing production company from the humblest of fringe theatre groups, success at the Royal Court Theatre, have all been achieved 'despite' the dominant cultural climate in Wales, not because of it. Thomas goes so far as to suggest that this is a positive thing, widening the argument out to embrace he new generation of young Welsh bands so beloved of the music press at the moment; they have, he argues, 'made up' a new Wales in spite of the dead hand of old arguments about cultural identity. Both Evans and Thomas are at great pains to want their words to be read as upbeat, "This interview should really be about celebration. Anything, but complaint." There is a real sense of wanting to move on from a Wales continually at war with itself about things that are of little interest to the rest of the world.

And yet... 'despite' themselves, both men acknowledge throughout the interview the obstacles and the lack of will which they encountered in the five years it took to make *House*. At one point Thomas says "There was a time when I would have cheerfully spat over every broadcaster in Wales, but not now" and later "We can sell cinema films abroad and we could have a structure similar to David Rose's Film on Four. It's starting to happen now with some of the BBC and S4C's ideas on distribution, but it's twelve or thirteen years behind." Throughout, there is an understandable tension between their relish for a culture that breeds imaginations forged through an oppositional sensibility and annoyance at the fact that as Thomas sees it "for years we [Wales] were internationally a laughing stock because we had no strategy for films." An age old tension in fact between the notion of the artist as romantic, maverick rebel and that of there being systems for nurturing and educating new voices, and providing outlets for them to be heard as part of any culture's desire to express itself in a wider context.

In certain key ways it is perhaps possible to see *House of America's* history as highly representative both of recent Welsh film and television history and, to an extent, of British film in general. It started its life looking to television as a source of finance, went through something of a mincing machine of misunderstanding and incomprehension, turned to European partnership and ended up grateful to the Lottery despite, as Marc Evans says, deep regrets over its political genesis. It has also become part of a generation of British cinema that has, as Ed Thomas puts it, produced 'back of beyond' films. Evans cites films from the English 'regions' such as *Butterfly Kiss* and *Boston Kickout* as well as the better known Scottish work and we can now of course add the bizarre international success of *The Full Monty*.

So are we to conclude finally that *House of America*, forged through adversity, heralds a new Welsh sensibility or was it a happy accident produced by determined individuals. It seems in the end that Evans and Thomas themselves are undecided, despite being better placed than most to assess any changes that may or may not have taken place during the time it took to make their film. Even the last words of the interview are torn between the optimistic assessment of the present – "It really is a different Wales now. Matthew Rees, a young actor who comes out of RADA with lots of prizes; his first three jobs: he does *House of America* in his own accent. Then he does a second television film in the Welsh language. Third he walks into the National Theatre and does a Peter Gill play about Cardiff in his own accent again. He will have no idea about the difference between that experience and what it was like for someone just ten years older" – and in the next sentence implicit doubts about the permanence of any such change or the ability of the arts establishment to respond to it – "This change hasn't been created by the establishment or any strategy, though it might have happened faster if there had been one. It's happened through accidents and desire."

The chapter on the impact on Wales of the arrival of digital broadcasting by Stuart Allan, Tom O'Malley and Andrew Thompson makes largely sobering reading, particularly for those most concerned with S4C's role in fostering a new sense of national identity during the last two decades. The authors, who have published elsewhere on the historical role of the print media in the evolution of Welsh identity, are concerned above all about the lack of urgent debate in Wales about the potential impact of digital. There is a sense that while many, including other contributors to this volume, are tentatively celebrating a resurgence of new Welsh fictions, there is a new monster waiting in the wings that has the potential to destroy a lot of what has been gained, particularly for those most concerned with broadcasting in the Welsh language.

The authors interestingly point out how in Wales much of the coverage of the coming of digital has been on the business pages nd there has been a distinct lack of any coverage of its potential wider cultural impact. These questions are not of course confined to Wales and the authors clearly demonstrate that their concerns are more fundamentally about the survival of public service broadcasting itself. But for many S4C, for all its faults, is one of the surviving minor miracles of a public service age and its ability to continue to have an impact has a special resonance for those interested in broadcasting beyond its potential to make large profits for the shareholders of television companies.

Ironically, as Allan, O'Malley and Thompson point out, S4C themselves are being generally upbeat about their role in a digital future having secured the contract to operate the Multiplex 3 television service. This will, for the first time, mean the availability of S4C across the UK and internationally via satellite. It will also enable the channel to expand into a whole range of new services that go well beyond its current remit. It is perhaps understandable then that some have seen digital as an exciting chance for "a totally Welsh company that reaches out into the world" as one spokesman puts it, to play a key role in establishing an identity for Wales in the age of the Assembly.

The authors though are sceptical. Digital will unleash market forces onto the Welsh broadcasting scene that could be the undoing of S4C in its own backyard. This then has the potential to reduce its role to simply another provider of the kind of pap that we already have more than enough of on terrestrial day-time television, never mind when we have around ninety channels of the stuff. Allan, O'Malley and Thompson put it succinctly and starkly when they say: "Despite the upbeat rhetoric being generated by S4C's spokespeople about its digital future, it is far from clear whether it will be able to continue to fulfil its remit in a multi channel world."

Dave Berry's survey of recent television fiction in Wales is as comprehensive as everybody familiar with his writing and archive work would expect. It is also scrupulously fair and even handed when passing judgement on an area that has come in for very severe recent criticism from both inside and outside Wales. The overwhelming sense though is of failure and lost opportunity.

As many have concluded before him, Berry sees that a fundamental cause of this failure has been a marked unwillingness to invest in Welsh drama and perhaps worse still a failure to acknowledge that there are voices that come out of Wales worthy of a network showing. The problem of the perception that 'the Welsh have S4C' has already been alluded to and its impact on the development of English language television drama in Wales has been very severe.

Dave Berry's assessment is perhaps most severe on the BBC, though its tone is very much more in sorrow than in anger. During the writing of this volume the drama department in Llandaff lost the latest of its heads, Karl Francis, after less than eighteen months in the job. It was perhaps his departure and the surrounding context that best sum up the recent history of BBC drama production in Wales; for many, Francis was always an unlikely appointment to a key institutional position with his track record as a strong oppositional film-maker in the tradition of a Loach or an Alan Clark. If his agenda was to succeed it would take not only a radical shake up of the Welsh department, but also for him to convince London to take Wales seriously and to view it as having similar potential as a source of strong popular drama to that of Scotland or Northern Ireland. Dave Berry's analysis strongly suggests that a failure to do the latter was the principal reason for Francis' departure, that and the detrimental draining impact of his new role on his own creativity:

Eighteen months later the optimism had drained away. Francis departed after achieving little. He left complaining (like his predecessors) of the BBC's alleged intractability and intransigence and lack of faith in Welsh initiated projects....

Again and again in Berry's account there is evidence that the BBC in London had become so dismissive of drama produced in Wales over the last two decades that even when it commissioned material originated there it was often at pains to minimise either Welsh involvement or any sense of a Welsh identity. This tendency included the frequent casting of non-Welsh leads in scarce 'prestige' drama (Kevin Whately, Dawn French, Alan Bates), the use of non-Welsh directors on series such as *Oliver's Travels* (1994) and even, according to Berry, the watering down of any sense of place in the promising detective series *Harper and Iles*.

At the time of writing it remains to be seen whether the track record of Pedr James (the current head of drama in BBC Wales) on such work as *Our Friends In The North* can carry any more weight in London than that of Francis. The signs are of an energetic search for new writing and there has been a considerable increase in the department's staffing in areas such as script development. It is to be hoped that this will soon result in work that can finally gain Cardiff the kind of respect currently afforded the drama departments in Glasgow and Belfast.

If the record of the BBC in Wales is depressing then that of HTV has been even worse, Berry asserts. Perhaps it is sympathy with the company's fate as one of the worst sufferers at the hands of Margaret Thatcher's franchise-bidding round that stops Berry being quite as hard on HTV as he is on the BBC. Despite this, he has some fairly scathing things to say about its "sheer failure of imagination" in almost opting out of drama origination altogether:

...the channel has soaked up an (admittedly pitiful) drama budget in such dubious exercises as recording the Sherman [Cardiff repertory theatre] series of lunchtime plays. These have, generally, been spectacularly uninteresting and even attempts to open out the material in constricting formats and studio settings have resulted in some embarrassing work. Until recently, HTV have failed English language drama in Wales miserably....

The "until recently" is another of the small signs of hope with which we beegan this volume. Under a new Head, Peter Edwards, HTV are working on a valleys-based long-running drama and encouragingly show signs of wanting to use young local talent to write and storyline it; they have a number of single drama projects which are slated for theatrical release before broadcast and currently seem at least as active as the BBC in trying to demonstrate that Wales has a small, but strong pool of writing talent. Again we wait in hope, but there are grounds for optimism.

When Berry turns his attention to S4C's record on drama one senses the same understandable reluctance to judge that has characterised much writing on the channel since its inception. The struggle for the channel to exist at all was so remarkable and its symbolic status so powerful that to criticise its lack of ambition in creating new Welsh fictions has been genuinely difficult.

There is now little disagreement though that S4C's early drama output was a grave disappointment with its stress on, as Berry says, "costume pieces and early drama" leading to accusations from even its own protégés like Stephen Bayly that it was totally pre-occupied with the folkloric and bucolic. It is also Berry's contention though that from the mid-eighties on, there have been uneven but welcome signs of a willingness to engage with contemporary subjects and even occasionally to encourage the taking of formal risks. He cites the success outside Wales of Karl Francis' *Boy Soldier* and Bayly's *Coming Up Roses* as the turning point (in 1986 they became the first two Welsh feature films to play simultaneously in the West End), though his account is certainly not one of unbroken progression from then on. Even recently he cites examples of the channel being tempted back onto conservative territory "in deference to its core audience," often encouraged by good viewing figures for unchallenging work.

And yet... work in television drama for S4C has fostered directors working in Welsh who have begun to make an impact on a wider stage. The Oscar nomination for Paul Turner's *Hedd Wynn* is only the best known tale; Endaf Emlyn, whose *Un Nos Ola Leuad (One Full Moon)* Berry calls "arguably the finest film ever to be made for television in Wales"; Ceri Sherlock (*Branwen, Cameleon*) and even Marc Evans who has recently worked predominantly in English, all have reason to be grateful for the existence of S4C. Above all perhaps the channel has been the main reason why some feel that Wales has an 'industry' at all; without S4C there would have been no reason for the growth of an independent sector on the scale that exists in Wales. Whilst agreeing with Dave Berry and others that this sector has not as yet produced the diversity of work that its size and composition promises, the very fact of its existence with its small army of skilled workers, experienced producers and directors may yet be one of the reasons why a distinctive Welsh film and television industry remains a possibility.

Daryl Perrins' 'This Town Ain't Big Enough For The Both Of Us' is both a comprehensive analysis of (like it or not) one of the most important films to come out of Wales in the past decade, *Twin Town,* and a wide-ranging piece of polemic on contemporary Welsh culture. Like its principal subject it is not afraid of sacred cows and will clearly not please everybody.

One of its starting points (already alluded to earlier in this introduction) is that *Twin Town's* critical reception both within the British film establishment and here in Wales completely misses the film's satirical point. Worse than this perhaps it totally misjudges the generic tradition to which the film belongs. His re-assessment sees *Twin Town's* natural ancestors as the best of the *Carry On* series, and as a critic he allies himself with those who see Sid, Hattie and Kenneth as true iconoclasts who also understand the audience they seek to address. For stuffy British institutions like the army, schools and hospitals, read the Welsh cultural establishment.

Perrins' argument is also useful and provocative in its irreverent placing of *Twin Town* in relation to other recent filmic visions of working class life amidst the wastelands of 'ex-industrial' Britain. It compares the almost sacred reverence for the brass band in *Brassed Off* with the bleak vision of the male voice choir in *Twin Town* and perhaps even more tellingly compares the latter's treatment of the 'sex industry' and its unlikeliest recruits with *The Full Monty*:

...in perhaps the darkest scene in *Twin Town*, the glamour of proletarian flesh, constructed by *The Full Monty*, is stripped bare to reveal the soulless, economic exchange underneath, as an overweight middle-aged masseuse matter-of-factly runs through her repertoire while puffing on a cigarette.

For Perrins, *Twin Town* is, for all its faults, one of the bravest of the British films of the 'nineties, daring to present a much bleaker, cruder and in his analysis funnier vision of contemporary underclass existence than any of its other commercially successful contemporaries.

It is of course in Wales itself that Kevin Allen's film has come in for some of its fiercest criticism and in this regard Perrins sees it in another noble Welsh cultural tradition, best represented for him by Caradoc Evans' *My People*. In a passage explicitly linking the two he says:

> Their popularity a barometer of conscious dissent against the establishment's continuous grand narrative of pretension, thus allowing feelings to surface that are commonly held, but rarely spoken, because they may be deemed disrespectful, fatalistic, unsavoury or even unpatriotic.

What starts as a re-appraisal of an important moment in the history of the recent Welsh film industry becomes also an overview of similar key moments in Welsh culture in the twentieth century. In Perrins' analysis *Twin Town* is rescued from being a second-rate *Trainspotting*, an opportunistic attempt to cash in on Celtic junkie chic, and instead a brave, flawed vision of Wales that is much more acutely aware of a particular vision of history than most were prepared to admit. In a comparison that is strangely moving, but which for some will be unpalatable, *Twin Town* is linked to one of the sacred moments of Welsh cinema; still discussing the massage parlour that figures so centrally in the film, Perrins says:

> The visual iconography is unsettling here, for as the masseuse leans over her client, arms outstretched, one is reminded of the still image of Rachel Thomas taken from *The Blue Scar* (1948) bending over her husband scrubbing his back in a bath next to the fire. A recurring image of Welsh womanhood to be found on book covers and at exhibitions across the land... the role and position are still intact, only the arena from domestic to business has changed.

In the end though there is hope in the film and this critical position if we can only recognise it, and Perrins implies that a healthy Welsh film culture must recognise this if it is to make progress:

> Perhaps we have now learnt to paraphrase Caradoc Evans, not to hate ourselves, but to like each other well enough to criticise our own behaviour.

Fizzy Oppe's piece is, like Phil John's, a powerfully personal account of the sheer difficulty (and occasionally the excitement) of working in the contemporary industry. It is also though an eloquent reminder of the importance of the short fiction film in any healthy film culture and perhaps especially so in a country like Wales.

The personal dimension to the piece is a valuable corrective to popular perceptions of a film-maker's existence and has strong links to Michelle Ryan's vision of the position of women in the Welsh industries. Alongside accounts of meetings with senior BBC executives is a litany of complicated and guilt-ridden childcare arrangements that will be depressingly familiar to anybody caring for children and trying to work in any demanding job. One is reminded of Derek Jarman's disarming honesty when talking about his freedom to remain true to a very personal vision in his films:

> It's because I'm gay. It's quite simple. Because I don't have any responsibility to family. All these other people are built in with mortgages, and have to find so many pounds a week to keep the kids clothed and I don't. I don't actually own anything and I've run the whole thing on debt.[17]

Leaving aside the important questions raised by Jarman's words, there remains an underlying issue, which Fizzy Oppe also addresses, about the kinds of voices that can be heard in film and television. Whilst New Labour rhetoric is all about providing the kinds of conditions in which women can (must!) work and have children, the film and television industry remains one of the most difficult of all within which to retain credibility and bring up children. This has important consequences for whose interpretations of the world we get to see and hear.

The other principal (though linked) dimension to Fizzy Oppe's piece is her foregrounding of the short film as an important force in contemporary Welsh film and television and indeed in the wider British industries. As she points out, Wales was very slow to recognise this in relation to Scotland and a number of the English regions, and it is arguable that this is one important factor in the comparatively slow growth of the Welsh film industry in general.

The last two or three years have seen initiatives within Wales that recognise the importance of the short film form both as a medium in itself and as an important arena for practitioners to develop and get their work shown. The PICS series (five short fiction films, produced by Fizzy Oppe) and the annual D.M. Davies Award at the Welsh International Film Festival (at £30,000 the biggest single prize for short film in Europe) have together helped foster a sympathetic climate in which short fiction can be made and seen in Wales, both in cinemas and on television. The importance of this building of a culture from the bottom up is immense and indeed already bearing fruit with the likes of Justin Kerrigan and Sara Sugarman launched on feature film careers, and other optimistic signals such as one of Fizzy Oppe's two 'Mad Housewives' being featured on *The Talent* as being amongst the most promising of young film-makers in Britain.

Short film though is not just about training for something greater, but a vital space in which alternative and independent voices can survive. One of the most depressing passages of Fizzy Oppe's piece recounts a BBC drama director saying "that he could see no point in making anything that less than 10 million people were going to watch. Anything less was an indulgence and a waste of licence payers' money". As the piece goes on to argue, there is now a demonstrable demand for 'minority' programming, for voices from beyond those who 'naturally' get to make television programmes, apart from anything else, and short film is a clear and obvious way to get those started in a hostile financial climate.

Fizzy Oppe's piece works on a number of different levels; it is partly a guide to hacking your way through the jungle of short film finance, partly an expression of frustration at the attitudes of so many in the mainstream business, but it is also finally a gesture of hope. As Fizzy herself claims, she is "no rookie producer out to make a name for myself, but a fairly hardened professional with twenty years film and television experience behind me"; this makes it all the more optimistic that she is prepared to argue and battle for low-budget short film and its special importance for under-represented voices.

Trying now to reflect on the overall tone of the contributions to this brief survey of a contemporary Wales on screen, one is to an extent struck by their variety, but it is also hard to escape the fact that the balance remains pessimistic. Arguably this is an unfashionable pessimism in the context of hopes for a new cultural direction given impetus by the Assembly and the various components of so-called 'Cool Cymru'. Again and again though, contributors draw attention to the *possibilities* apparent in the Welsh position only to then go on to give accounts of how these are wasted or thwarted, either by public policy makers or by the social and economic conditions created by the global industries.

Almost inevitably one returns to Ed Thomas's 'despite culture'; pockets of ideas, enthusiasm, occasional solid achievement mostly 'despite' the prevailing structures and conditions.

It would be distortion to suggest though that nothing is changing. On the face of it, both Channel 4 and the BBC in London are currently committed to more 'regional' drama and film production, and BBC Wales for one is attempting to respond through what appears a genuine trawl for new voices and faces. S4C's drama policy continues to shift just a little from the timidity of its first decade, and HTV at least appears to be interested in dramatic fictions again after abandoning (some would say after being forced to abandon) even a minimal commitment for a period in the early 1990s.

The setting up of Sgrîn and the political weight it ought to carry should at least send out some of the right signals even if the infrastructure for supporting feature film production still hasn't begun to approach the obvious Scottish model. Currently the priorities here seem to be about unearthing writers to connect with European scale projects such as *Moonstone* and equipping Welsh producers to develop projects along similar lines to their counterparts in other small-nation film cultures. What Sgrîn must be concerned with is developing the confidence that film is being thought about strategically in Wales and perhaps it is still too early to tell whether this has begun to happen. At least now Welsh applications to the Lottery for film funding are assessed in Wales instead of being sent to Scotland because of the perception that there wasn't the experience here!

Even if the key institutions remain in a state of flux, what certainly seems to have emerged during the last decade or so is recognition of the importance of moving images, alongside other contemporary cultural output, towards Wales' current political position. Moving images that are from Wales, and perhaps recognisably Welsh, but not exclusively locked within older ways of thinking about national identity.

Justin Kerrigan's *Human Traffic* arrived too close to the publication date for this book to consider it in much detail, but in key ways it is strongly suggestive of future directions which the national film industry may take. It has been discussed as a Welsh film and uses Cardiff as an effective and exhilarating back-drop, but it has more often been discussed as a film about a generation that just happens to have been made in Wales by a young Welshman. It is most definitely not interested in the more sterile debates about identity. In making it his 'film of the week,' *The Observer's* Philip French accurately saw *Human Traffic* as a clean break with an older Wales and instead saw its true antecedents as American, particularly early Scorsese, Bob Rafelson, Woody Allen and (almost inevitably!) Quentin Tarantino. The irony of course is that it took the money of *Irish Screen* to get the film made.

Even closer to our publisher's deadline and even further from any apparent burden of national representation has come Ed Thomas's directorial debut *Rancid Aluminium* – a wild romp through the comedy thriller genre with nods to a number of other American forms, including the Western, on the way.

Whatever its eventual critical reception, and the signs are that it will be decidedly mixed; the film at least looks like a characteristically bold attempt to consolidate the right of affirmedly Welsh artists to occupy territory well away from the homeland and to bring with them the perspective and confidence of a vibrant young country. The next twelve months promise more of the same with new features from Sara Sugarman, Philippa Cousins, Karl Francis and Christopher Monger.

If this book is to have a true value, it will make its contribution to the growing awareness of a powerful role for all the creative talents involved in film in Wales and add its voice to those who will urge policy makers not to ignore the so-called 'cultural industries' when faced with an array of more politically pressing priorities.

Notes

1. J. Hill, 'British Television and Film: The Making of a Relationship' in J. Hill and Martin McLoone, *Big Picture, Small Screen: The Relations Between Film and Television* (University of Luton Press: Luton, 1996) p.161.
2. A. Higson, in L. Friedman (ed), *British Cinema and Thatcherism* (University College of London Press: London, 1993).
3. J. Hill, *ibid*, p.164.
4. J. Caughie, in C. McArthur, *Scotch Reels: Scotland in Cinema and Television* (BFI: London, 1982) p.120.
5. Interview in *New Welsh Review* 27, 1994-5, p.61.
6. D. Adams, *Stage Welsh* (Gomer: Ceredigion, 1996).
7. See a number of the essays in McArthur (1982), *op.cit.*
8. B. Thompson, 'Twin Town' in *Sight and Sound*, volume 7, number 4, April 1997, p.53.
9. N. Morris, 'Projecting Wales' in *Planet* 126, December–January 1998, p.27.
10. D. Berry, 'Darkman' in *Orson* (Chapter Film Notes), November 1997.
11. D. Berry, *op cit.*
12. C. Monk, 'Darklands' in *Sight and Sound*, volume 7, number 11, November 1997, p.37.
13. L. Spencer, 'House of America' in *Sight and Sound*, volume 7, number 9, September 1997, p.45.
14. K. Rockett, Luke Gibbons and John Hill, *Cinema and Ireland*, (Routledge: London, 1988).
15. D. Berry, *Wales and Cinema, The First Hundred Years*, (University of Wales Press: Cardiff, 1994).
16. A. Calderwood, 'Film and Television Policy in Scotland' in J. Hill and Martin McLoone, *op.cit.*
17. D. Jarman, Interview in *New Musical Express*, 25 May, 1985.

A Woman's Place: Women and Film in Wales

Michelle Ryan

Thirty years after the arrival of women's liberation on this island and while apparently inhabiting a 'post-feminist' period, it might seem an opportune time to examine women's place in the film and TV industries in Wales. How far have we travelled? How successful have we been at achieving equality both in front of and behind the cameras? How have we improved the representation of women on the screen? Will we be entering the new century better equipped to take our place alongside men – will it matter if we don't?

It seems to me that the media is the terrain where these debates and struggles should find their sharpest focus? As Clare Johnston has said: "It has been at the level of the image that the violence of sexism and capitalism has been experienced". And it is at the level of image that we construct much of our personal identity, with film and TV offering us role models, heroes and heroines, idols and icons to people our dreams and fantasies, and mirror the world back to us. It is also at the level of the image that we are seeing a feminist backlash. Which is why as a producer and a consumer, I think it vital that women should have equal representation in front of and behind the camera and why it is important to revisit the recent history of women and their struggle to gain a place in the male dominated world of film and TV. Who knows, we might all live to see for the first time in Wales women taking their place in the Welsh media and the new Assembly not because they are token women, but because they represent and embody the significant contribution women have made to Wales over the years and because Wales needs their input to banish the sterility of much Welsh political and cultural life still under male domination.

Prior to the 1980s it was pretty difficult to associate women with film in Wales – not so much hidden from history as absent! Even the films made in Wales or about Wales often used English, Irish or American actresses to portray Welsh women. Who were the women in front of and behind the camera? Unfortunately not many names roll off the tongue. There was of course Rachel Thomas, a fine actress whose career spanned a diversity of roles. Rachel was a consummate professional who brought hard work, dignity and integrity to her roles in film, television, radio and stage.

Her 'Mam' characters embodied an era which is now merely a memory, when a woman's role in life remained firmly fixed within the domestic space. A matriarch in her own home, 'Mam' had little power or influence outside it. As Rachel said many times, she modelled her 'Mam' characters on her mother and grandmother and the many women she grew up with. She merely distilled those qualities into one character, partly an invention, but also a representation of many women's lives in Wales up until recently. As one critic said of her role in *Proud Valley,* she was, "the symbol of all miners' wives and daughters". These women might not have had much say in the world of politics, work and public life, but they were the absolute bedrock of family, community and chapel life.

As we tried to point out in the film *Mam* made by Red Flannel, these women were the unsung heroines of Welsh history, without whom the other archetype, the Welsh miner might never have existed, because they were mutually interdependent. She was the backbone of the family, creating something out of nothing, keeping a tidy house with the constant battle against dirt and disease, feeding and clothing a family on a tight budget and living through untold sacrifices to ensure her family survived. The flip side of this was of course the contribution these women made to constructing the Welsh man – helpless as a baby and totally dependent on the servicing of a woman for all his needs. It was the Welsh 'Mam' who also brought her daughters up to continue that servicing job and who contributed to the maintenance of a culture which kept men at the centre of the home and the community. Now Rachel Thomas has gone and that image of the Mam and the traditions that underpinned her have gone also, to exist only as a memory, captured for posterity on film. In reality Rachel's life was not that traditional. Although she may have looked the part, Rachel was a single, working mother when it was not easy, having been widowed at a relatively early age. And like many actresses in Wales, Rachel was critical of the lack of good roles for women and the chauvinism rife in her industry. In this age where women's lives have changed in Wales more significantly than men's, where there has been a revolution in women's working lives and where men are being forced to change by the same women who saw to their every need, Rachel embodied the best of both traditions. As an actress she was a model of professionalism to us all and as a woman she encompassed the best of Welsh womanhood – kindness, strength, calm determination and an abiding concern for others.

The darker side of what this culture can do to women is however embodied in the actress Rachel Roberts, an outstanding actress but a very troubled woman, whose decline into drunkenness and paranoia robbed us of a considerable talent. She represented at that time the female rebel who rejected the conformism of non-conformist Wales. In films like *Saturday Night and Sunday Morning, This Sporting Life, O Lucky Man,* as well as many strong performances on TV and theatre, she displayed intelligence and passion and a Welshness she never abandoned. In those days there was a price to pay for such rebellion, but she provided a role model for those of us who wanted to reject the destiny men had determined for us.

In television the situation was just as uninspiring. According to John Davies there were only four women in senior positions in the BBC during its first 60 years: they were Nan Davies, Mai Jones, Lorraine Davies and Teleri Bevan – *"a dismal record indeed"*.[1] Behind the camera the situation was even worse, in that the only woman associated with film before the 1980s in Wales was Jill Craigie. Not because she was Welsh, but because her film *Blue Scar* portrayed the valleys sympathetically and the woman had a career, although the content which focused on a love story and nationalisation was not so successful. Still, for women film-makers in the 'eighties starved of role models to relate to, it provided some inspiration.

It is not until the early 'eighties that we can see a significant sea change in this situation. When I returned to Cardiff in 1981, armed with a diploma in film, TV and radio production from Bristol University, I found a mainstream industry and a culture more entrenched in patriarchal attitudes than anything I had experienced in England. Like many other women at the time who were having difficulties getting a union ticket and breaking into the industry, I chose to work in the independent sector where there was at least some support and a sympathetic environment. In Cardiff this was Chapter Film Workshop where low budget independent film-making was going on, usually with some grant aided support from the Welsh Arts Council.

At the time there were quite a few women in the workshop, but nearly all of them played supporting roles to the men. Disgruntled by our marginalisation and encouraged by the work of women film-makers outside of Wales, we formed our own group in November 1981 called South Wales Women's Film Group (S.W.W.F.G.) – the first women in film organisation in Wales.

We formed the S.W.W.F.G. with the intention of sharing our skills, supporting our ideas and enabling women to play a more active part in film-making. We secured a small amount of money from the Welsh Arts Council and worked together on small film projects. This period saw a flowering of women's film groups outside London – Bristol, Sheffield, Leeds, York, Norwich and Nottingham which had emerged from various feminist movements and film-making organisations and were able to benefit from the decentralisation of arts funding and to address some of the issues raised by feminists like Laura Mulvey, Charlotte Brunsden and Pam Cooke. We were all involved in the IFA (Independent Film-makers Association) whose brief was to encourage the growth of a regional film culture, support a diverse range of film-makers from the experimental to the didactic, and lobby broadcasters and funding bodies to support the work we were all doing. Our activities in the S.W.W.F.G. were also underpinned by the two women's film distribution companies Circles and C.O.W. who could supply us with women's films from all over the world. Whilst the S.W.W.F.G. group didn't make many films because of the lack of funding, of the thirty or so members, over half gained enough training and support to enable them to work in film and TV related areas.

The first activity that resulted from the group was in May 1982 as part of a national 'Women Live' event. This was organised centrally from London with the aim of exhibiting all the different achievements of women in the arts and media. We decided to hold a month long 'Women's Film Event' in Chapter – an ambitious project, but a very successful one that clearly defined itself as the first feminist event in Wales. Over the month there were over 50 films shown at Chapter, the majority of them having been made by women over the previous ten years. In Cinema 1 there were two weeks of films about and for women and in Cinema 2, four programmes of films showing at the weekends. During the first week in Cinema 1 the programme included films made by men about women alongside short feminist films, to contrast how men view women and how women view themselves. The second week was based around the themes of women and work. In Cinema 2 the first weekend programme covered the development of British feminist film over the previous ten years including animation; the second was on sexuality, including a women-only event which erupted into controversy when a transvestite tried to attend and was forced to leave! The third weekend showed feminist films from Europe and Australia and the fourth weekend was devoted to the work of Bristol and Cardiff women film-makers.

The success of this season was followed up by organising the first national feminist film and video conference in April 1983, which brought women from all over the UK to Chapter in Cardiff to discuss the nature of female/feminist film, the industry, distribution, exhibition, film making practice, feminist film criticism, funding and networking. Both events sparked off a lot of interest in women making films, encouraged a number of women to press on with their media ambitions and secured a significant amount of support from the W.A.C.

At the time, a lot of the women chose to work in documentary because it allowed them to address key issues concerning women and it was cheaper and easier to make than fiction. Many women viewed fiction as fixing women in a 'compromised' position within an inherently sexist narrative structure.

The protagonist was inevitably male which left women as an appendage, a threat, a sex object, or dead!

Equally there was a process of using film to explore how we saw ourselves as women and how we wanted to be represented. Through the I.F.A. in Wales, we could also collaborate with and support other women working in Wales in areas like Swansea, Aberystwyth, Bangor and Wrexham. Out of the S.W.W.F.G. emerged a women's history group which also made a short film on the suffragettes around work that Deirdre Beddoe was doing and which led to a similar group in Swansea.

It therefore seemed a natural extension of our work and ideas to become involved in the miners strike and in particular to support the women. At various stages we all attended meetings, demonstrations and pickets lines and collaborated on a project documenting women's role in the strike called *Not Just Tea and Sandwiches* produced at the Video Workshop in Cardiff and made our own video called *Something Else in the House* which grew out of working with various miners' support groups, screening films and helping to raise funds.

The success of these initiatives encouraged a small group of us – Frances Bowyer, Clare Richardson, Carol White and myself to form a women's film workshop, which we set up in Pontypridd and which we hoped would become a Channel 4 franchised film workshop. In those days it was very difficult to become a member of the union and therefore difficult to get a job. What Channel 4 offered was the possibility of a network of film and video workshops throughout the country providing a programme of work for Channel 4 which would be innovative, empowering, often experimental, and very closely tied to their communities.

As a Channel 4 workshop you had union recognition, a three year period where C4 would provide equipment and capital to run a workshop, provide four full-time salaries and fund a programme of work that would incorporate local initiatives and at least one broadcast programme a year. A workshop's brief was therefore to encourage the representation of regional, ethnic and gender identities on TV and facilitate the expression of new voices and experiences previously not available to TV and its audiences. Surprisingly we were successful, forming a women's

Channel 4 workshop called Red Flannel. Much had been written about the history of working class struggle in Wales, but very little about the contribution women made to it. Constance Wall Holt in her huge bibliography on Welsh women suggests that women's history in Wales "has been buried just as surely as the rich veins of coal were buried in the valleys of Wales. Layers of conscious government and cultural policy and discrimination have buried the stories deep". She goes on to say that, "Welsh women have been described as 'culturally invisible.' Their history has been buried under layers of intentional oppression of the Welsh and conscious or unconscious discrimination against women".[2]

Red Flannel saw one of its primary functions as helping to uncover that history of Welsh women within the valleys, both in terms of their domestic activity (the reproduction and maintenance of labour power) and their public life (their role in chapels, women's organisations and political parties as well as in the community).

Another function was to document the period of transition that the valleys' communities were undergoing as a result of the decline of mining and heavy industry and the recruitment of many more women into employment, and to focus on issues of importance to women in the valleys as defined by them at the point of contact with Red Flannel.

With funding from Channel 4 and supported by further grants from W.A.C., S.E.W.A.A. (South East Wales Arts Association) and the E.O.C. (Equal Opportunities Commission), Red Flannel was able to develop an integrated practice of work that, besides making at least one hour of broadcast material a year, also had a programme of work which involved us working with women's groups in the valleys' communities. We worked with women on many of the estates in the valleys, like Penrhys estate, where we helped them produce their own video to promote a more positive image of the estate and a reply to the massacre they received from the media and BBC Wales in particular.

We also trained a number of women in video and computing skills, as well as providing them with the confidence and presentation skills to be more ambitious for themselves and their communities and we ran training courses for community organisations to help them pass on their skills to the groups they were working with, as in Rhydfelin estate near Pontypridd where they produced a tape documenting how they had set up a very effective credit union to combat the loan sharks. We also provided a cultural facility in a number of areas by running film clubs which in a very small way compensated for the lack of cinemas in the area.

Our first film, *Mam* was about the role women had played in the mining communities of the South Wales valleys. When we started to research it we were shocked to find how little source material was available. Lengthy visits to the Miners Library only produced interviews with women about their fathers and sons and almost nothing about women's role in Welsh history – evidence yet again of how much of women's experiences and stories had been hidden from history, lost from the collective memory. In fact women have always played an active role in the transmission of culture – telling stories, passing on rituals and traditions, creating myths, verbally constructing imaginary worlds for their children. And yet in this age of communication where all the tests show girls' communication skills are more sophisticated than boys, they are still such a minority in the media.

The high point of all this work was the first screening of *Mam* at the Parc and Dare in Treorchy. The place was packed for a screening of a documentary film about women and made by women. The response was tremendous and inspirational for ourselves and for many of the women who had become involved in the making of the film. As soon as it was completed it was leapt on by schools and colleges desperate to have some source material. It was also chosen for the Edinburgh Film Festival, purchased by the British Film Council and shown all over the world. At the time we thought we were contributing to opening the space up for women in Wales and that in 5-10 years time women would have real equality and we would see women's lives being represented in history, literature, culture and the media, as well as attracting more women into working in the media. Madly optimistic and in retrospect naive, but the arrival of Channel 4 and the difference it made to television, carried us all away on a wave of optimism at least until the bubble burst and its commercial teeth got a lot sharper.

Today we can see the benefits and fall-out from this period. Certainly there are now a number of female producers and directors and even some women working in the technical sphere as editors, camerawomen and sound recordists. There are one or two women who have broken through the glass ceiling in the industry and a W.F.T.V.N. (Women in Film and Television Network) organisation[3] that tries to keep the issue of women on the agenda. Today there are many more talented actresses working through the medium of Welsh and English although they still complain about the lack of good scripts and challenging parts.

Every broadcaster has to have certain equality targets and the heads of drama at BBC, HTV and S4C all seem to be trying hard to encourage women writers and find women's stories. There is also a healthy independent production sector in Wales which amounts to between 50-70 companies. Here you will find a significant number of women acting as producers, directors, owners of companies and executives. There are even a few companies which consist of a majority of women. The freelance world is not particularly conducive to women with its insecurities and scant employment protection, but what it can offer is freedom from the male dominated hierarchical structures of the broadcasting institutions and therefore more opportunities to express their talent and skills.

So things have improved – slightly! But why are these men still so difficult to shift? Why do we see and hear so much on film, TV and radio that is still about *their* pre-occupations? Why do we have only a handful of women in the top jobs in broadcasting? Why are most of the scripts still written by men? It is nearly thirty years since women started campaigning for equal rights and opportunities – surely that's long enough for even Wales to have caught on to the idea that if women are involved you get a whole new perspective and source of energy being represented? Has the impact of post-feminism so successfully muted women's anger and frustration that even when faced with an objective reality that is still not in their favour, they prefer not to appear too critical in case they are seen as uncool, anti-men, un-feminine – a threat? And what an irony that the media, which has done so much for post-feminism, using every opportunity to point out that women have 'arrived' and there is no longer any need for feminism; has perhaps one of the worst records when it comes to employing and representing women. Perhaps we will have to accept that the indecent haste to embrace post-feminism has been premature.

We also need to reiterate for the sake of the younger generation of women that things have improved too slowly and that the slightest let up on the pressure and men soon forget about the arguments for including women and rapidly return to that exclusive male culture in which they feel secure, where the only visible women are those who help to ease their passage through life.

This is still a problem not just in Wales but throughout Europe. In a number of equality surveys done in the last few years the same picture is represented. Out of 79 broadcasting organisation in 12 states one out of every 1000 women was at the top, compared with one out of every 140 men. 76% of women fall into the lower half of the pay hierarchy in all divisions and only 10% of women occupy top positions. In the UK only 6 out of 61 board members of ITV companies are women and in 1994 all prime-time commissioning editors at BBC and ITV were men. In Wales the BBC had to reach a target by 2000 of 40% women in middle management, which they seem to have achieved, and 30% of women in top management, which they don't look like meeting. HTV did have Menna Richards at the top but the overall figure is between 10-15% at senior management level. In S4C the picture is slightly better but again nowhere near 50% at senior management and commissioning levels. Added to that is the trickle-down effect where men tend to select men so that the creative personnel further down the hierarchy who are producing and directing are in the main men as well, inevitably producing a TV service heavily skewed towards men's interests. So despite all the changes in women's lives in the last fifteen years, very little of it is seen on Welsh screens. The masculine is still the norm of desire. It still acts as the main reference point, still defines the dominant gaze, still views women as marginal, and it is still an industry dominated by male producers and female consumers.

Perhaps it is no surprise that we are seeing a more encouraging development in the appearance of a new generation of women film-makers in Wales who have been able to resist the demands of TV and to concentrate on film-making; women like Sarah Sugarman, Catrin Clarke, Margaret Constantas, Phillipa Cousins, Karen Rees, Jane Hubbard, Joanne Quinn, Catherine Linstrum; from the artistic to the commercial, they are producing films that bring a woman's perspective to film and offer something different from the young, male, 'rites of passage' films that seem to dominate the circuit. What Channel 4 and S4C generated in the 1980s was a significant shift of film-makers out of the independent sector as it was then known, into television. In the late 1990s we are beginning to see a reversal of that trend. As a result of the lottery, the popularity of British films, broadcasters funding feature films, the growth of film courses and the increasing interest in and support of short films, we are seeing a rapid expansion of the film industry even in Wales. I hope that at least some of this new generation of women film-makers will help to produce a Welsh cinema that can speak to us all.

As someone who loves the cinema and all the pleasures it offers, I look forward to the added pleasure waiting for me when cinema expresses women's experience. Then I would have the same thrill of recognition that I see men relishing when they go and see one of the many films addressing their experience, from the phallic Rambo hero to football, from music to mercenaries, from heart-throb to terminator – so much is about them. Not surprising, given the industry is still heavily male dominated. And before anyone rushes forward with the argument that there is nothing stopping women, in fact there is. One is the obvious lack of role models in the director stakes – it is getting better, but they are still more noticeable as exceptions. Then, the over-emphasis on technology and the mechanical art of film-making rather than the visual and verbal has inevitably excluded all but the most dedicated of women. Added to which women's stories and female directors are not seen as very marketable.

Our small country needs a good film industry to act as an ambassador, a trade promoter and a mirror. For a relatively small amount of money it can make a real impact. Creating positive images for women and enabling them to work in the media depends on making a space for them. We have to carry on demanding more space in our culture and more opportunities to re-define, retrieve and re-examine many aspects of it. To do this we have to feel proud of what we can offer, we have to find ways of realising our potential, we have to convince the commissioners and funders that our stories are just as compelling as men's. Finally, we have to feel strongly that the things we care about, the future we want for our children, the community we want to live in, the men we want to share our lives with and the specific Welshness of that experience are all worth working and fighting for. And if they are worth that amount of effort, they are also worth representing in our films and on our television.

Notes

1. John Davies, *Broadcasting and the BBC in Wales*, (University of Wales Press: Cardiff, 1994).
2. Constance Wall Holt, *Welsh Women: An annotated bibliography of Women in Wales and Women of Welsh descent in America,* (The Scarecrow Press Inc.: 1993).
3. A national organisation with its head office in London. Its main task is to lobby the industry in an effort to improve the employment of women and to argue for better working conditions. There is a branch in Wales based in Cardiff.

The Story of a Welsh Screenplay
Philip John

This piece was written in 1997. In the interim period there have been some encouraging developments for English language drama in Wales. I have outlined these at the end.

The following essay is divided into two parts: 'Boxing Shadows' and 'Punch Drunk.' 'Boxing Shadows' sets the context for the English-speaking writer working within Wales. It discusses some of the problems inherent in the creation of a viable Welsh film industry from the perspective of the screenwriter. It attempts to give a flavour of the area and culture I draw upon in my writing and introduces the screenplay that springs from my experience of growing up in the south Wales valleys.

'Punch Drunk' is a series of informal extracts taken from my work journal charting the course of *The Kissing Ghost* screenplay over the course of four years.

Boxing Shadows
Introduction.

It is customary in certain parts of India for a wedding celebration to be gatecrashed by a couple of eunuchs dressed in women's clothing. These 'Invisibles' or 'hijras' get very drunk and harangue the guests. Their activities are met with a mixture of tolerant amusement and total indifference. Indian eunuchs belong to a caste so low as to be practically unseen. Unfettered from the protocols and conventions of Indian Society, the 'Invisibles' are free to wreak havoc. This 'freedom' however presupposes that the wreaking of havoc is to be regarded by eunuchs as the only ambition worth having since, marginalised by society, they are free to do little else.

The English language Welsh writer is the Welsh broadcasting equivalent of the 'hijra.' The communities, the stories, the authentic language of contemporary English speaking Wales, *Satellite City* being a recent and notable exception, are barely represented on our screens.

BBC Wales' long practised disregard for the hordes of shadow-punching Welsh 'hijras' has no doubt contributed to its failure to appeal to the Network. Compare BBC Wales' output with that of BBC Scotland, whose extensive Network presence is characterised by diversity and inclusivity.

BBC Scotland's present high profile on the Network owes much to the quality of its heads of drama. Bill Bryden (*Tutti Frutti, Play On One, Taking Over The Asylum*) and current incumbent Andrea Calderwood (*The Crow Road, Hamish Macbeth, Cardiac Arrest*) have laid the foundations for a generation of bold, culturally assertive Scottish film-makers.

How do we develop and support new Welsh actors, writers and directors? One way is to put them to work. It is part of the role of the broadcaster to find indigenous talent able to deliver quality contemporary Welsh drama. Karl Francis attempted a radical change in departmental infrastructure and programming policy during his short spell as head of drama at BBC Wales. I would like to see Pedr James, Karl's successor, and Peter Edwards at HTV, build on this idea of inclusivity and create the conditions for a new school of bold, original and relevant English language Welsh programming.

If we are to develop a new generation of film-makers it is important to remind ourselves that cinema and television are very distinct and separate art forms. Cinema is an epic art form, which, in its purest form, tells stories with pictures. Television obeys different grammar, different punctuation, different phrasing. Television drama is a truly fantastic medium with the potential to reach into the living rooms of millions. However, this miraculous tool is so often blunted. Bad television drama has been described as 'radio with pictures,' compromised by the broadcaster's dictum that its messages, images and signs need to be absolutely clear, obvious and direct. Bad cinema on the other hand takes on the appearance of high quality television. When viewing new British films it is disconcerting to see how pervasive and insidious the techniques and aesthetic of our terrestrial media have become. Perhaps, as the necrotising influence of digital TV eats away at production budgets and British television output begins to resemble that of its European counterparts, the difference between the small and the big screen will become more clearly defined. Maybe then our cinema will rid itself of demonic possession by 'Quality Television Drama' and regenerate itself into a unique art form of grand themes, ideas and dreams.

In the meantime, a host of fresh new shadows have come jinking and southpawing over the horizon. We have a new government, a Welsh Assembly, two new Heads of Drama and last but not least, the much vaunted Welsh media agency. Accuse any of these of ignoring or refusing to nurture the 'hijras', and they'll throw their gloved fists into the air claiming that the times they are a-changing and new plans are afoot. In the meantime, we 'Invisibles' stagger from wedding party to commissioner to consultation meeting, and life goes on. Nothing changes.

It is important to be optimistic that the Welsh film establishment will find some way out of its current inertia. Such optimism does require an incredible leap of faith. In the past our efforts towards creating a viable film industry have been so woefully inadequate.

One case in point is the now defunct Welsh Film Council. Apart from the PICS scheme – four short films for theatrical release commissioned from new Welsh writers and directors – its achievements were scant. It was hindered by an annual production budget of peanuts – sixty thousand pounds – and a total lack of political will on the part of its board to lobby for more Welsh Office funding.

Sgrîn, the new Welsh media agency is to commence operations in spring 1998. It is to become responsible for the administration of Welsh lottery funding, and the dispersal of film production grants totalling sixty thousand pounds. One hopes that Sgrîn will encourage transparency in the way it operates and invite local practitioners onto its management board. One would also hope that the agency employs experienced cine-literate script readers with the kind of imagination and vision required for recognising and encouraging indigenous talent. In the dark and dreadful past, the people best suited to work of this kind were either too busy with projects of their own, or else wilfully ignored. For what it's worth, I would like to see a strong bias towards script development incorporated into the agency's production strategy.

English language Welsh film-makers are well accustomed to finding ways of eking out a living to enable them to devote time to the quaint-bordering-on-masochistic hobby of screenwriting. The problem of finding enough money to live whilst writing is one faced by most new screenwriters. Producers will not risk development money on a new writer when they have no guarantee the script will even be completed, let alone be good enough to finance. Development funding is the hardest money to access. But then, without a script there can be no film.

Sgrîn could provide financial and practical support, perhaps most usefully to a limited slate of projects not yet attached to a production company. The development scheme should incorporate provision for the services of a credible, industry standard script editor experienced in working with screenplays for cinema. Within the production strategy I would also like to see the introduction of an annual PICS scheme, and a level of film production funding sufficient to finance the production of films.

An effective Film Board would play its part in the creation of a viable Welsh film industry. However, making films for theatrical release is an entrepreneurial venture. Wales has a number of dynamic, independent producers with the passion and the sensibility to create films that will perform in the global arena.

We also have to consider the question of cultural self-confidence. We are all aware of the metropolitan prejudice of certain elements in the London-centric press quick to portray Wales as 'dull', 'un-sexy' and 'unimaginative.' A.N. Wilson's claim that the Welsh have "never made a significant contribution to any branch of knowledge, culture and entertainment" is a case in point.

Welshness is an elastic and complex concept. The word itself derives from the Anglo-Saxon word for 'foreigner'. My sense of 'nationhood' derives from an upbringing in a few streets in a particular valley. Our country has never, apart from short isolated periods, been a united one. Wales is fragmented – historically, linguistically and geographically. It was hardly surprising then to witness the kind of apathy, uncertainty and division made manifest by the referendum for the Welsh Assembly. Personally, I see these fault lines as a source of vitality, strength and inspiration.

However, a culture continually gazing at its own navel, ever obsessed with the need to state its own existence, doubting its right just to *be* is already cold in the grave. The selection panel for the Celtic Film Festival once turned down a film of mine on the basis that it wasn't 'Welsh enough'. "Good film, but could've been made anywhere." What does a Welsh film look like?

To answer that question let us consider the work of Canadian auteur Atom Egoyam. His films are dense, challenging, deeply-rooted in his personal experience and brimming with contemporary ideas and themes with little or no reference to the cultural baggage of their country of origin. His work is considered no less 'Canadian' for all that. So what does a Welsh film look like? It looks like a film.

If Welsh film is not well represented in world cinema, it is not because the world is against us. It is because we are failing. We must learn to write better scripts, make better films and market them effectively.

The Worried Well

I grew up in a small stretch of the Ebbw Valley in South Wales during the sixties. Pontywaun was a working class village more swingeing than swinging. The river Ebbw at that time was one of the most polluted waterways in Britain. We could tell the time of day by the colour of the water; it ran carbon black until lunchtime and ferrous orange until four o'clock. Teatime was signalled by a floating armada of Sunblest loaves from the bakery.

Anglo-Welsh writer Gwyn Thomas once described an upbringing in the South Wales valleys as "a pungent compost of early mutilations". The river, the quarry, the woods, the tip, the knotweed, the canal and the railway line. These places were the perfect antidote to the tomb-like interiors of Home. The hills were alive with porn, stripping girls, the *worried well*, tramps, misfits, and the insane: Young Birt, soft in the head, who bludgeoned his true love on Trinity Hill; Spooner Jones, who, having buried his donkey in a hole that was too shallow, took a hacksaw to its legs; and Shilling, the laughing one-toothed giant, who lived rough by the canal.

Immaculate front rooms were temples to Banality, where the sacraments included neurotic manias, domestic dysfunction and surreally libidinous longings. Dad's bookshelf was crammed with horror stories, encyclopaedias on witchcraft, Japanese war atrocities and strange photographs of nude women with no genitalia (airbrushed for decency). Mam used to insist that the 'healthy mottling' on my legs was all the cabbage she ate whilst pregnant with me. It was also Mam who told me that sunlight contained vitamins. The bleak and absurd poetry of the mundane continues to influence the way I look at the world.

Ours was and is a community with its own poetry, its own rhythms and nuances, its own 'living language'. My relationship with the Welsh language, which also has its own poetry and rhythms, but which makes much of its cultural and historic pedigree, is that of the bastard son. After all, Welsh was never taught in my school, and never spoken on the streets. To learn Welsh now would be an act of cultural dishonesty, a denial of my history as an 'hijra,' an attempt to ingratiate myself with the wedding guests. Cultural dishonesty is a state of self-consciousness, the antithesis of free expression.

The Kissing Ghost

I always knew what I wanted to say. The problem was how to say it. It was whilst at Newport Film School, guided and encouraged by writer/director Steve Gough and Head of Department, Les Mills, that I had the idea for my first feature script.

The official pitch begins like this:

The story is set in a village on the South Wales coast in a parallel 1969. Polar ice caps are melting and global warming has turned Wales into a semi-tropical dustbowl. Rising seas and rapacious tides are threatening global economic stability. A plan is hatched to stop the tides by blowing up the moon. The explosive devices are set. The countdown begins. The world waits...

Arthur Barbaro, the hero of the story is an emotionally constipated four-teen-year-old who has a recurring nightmare of a ghost that smothers him with a kiss. He loves Jessie, a girl from the village. Arthur lives with his devouring and emotionally frigid mother, Alice. Her armoury of mind

control techniques includes the warning that Arthur's youthful erections are
a warning to run home as he has wandered into 'invisible clouds of germs.'
As a result Arthur is unable to be with Jessie long enough to woo her.
The moon blows. The village celebrates. Natural cycles begin to unravel.
People are behaving strangely. Alice has begun to menstruate once again. A
strange nymphomania overcomes her. Arthur, once entirely overwhelmed by
Alice, is left alone to make sense of a disintegrating world... (With comic,
murderous, carnal, tragic, results)

Reduced to a sentence the idea looks like this:

An ironic, emotionally turbulent and darkly comic science fiction in
which a young boy tries to find his way in a world of inertia, sex and cata-
strophe.

The problems I encountered when I set out to write my first
feature script are ones, I believe, shared by many new writers,
whether they care to admit to them or not.

For me, the prospect of turning one sentence into a ninety-
page script was so daunting I blindly refused to acknowledge the
size of the task. I had a lot of ideas, perhaps too many. I didn't
write a treatment, or a plan. I simply began writing. I would
reach page thirty, decide there was a more interesting way to
start the film, then begin again. I must have reworked those first
thirty pages eight or ten times. The fact was, I was choosing to
return to the start because I didn't know where the story went
beyond page thirty.

Looking back, part of the problem lay with my way of writing. I had always worked intuitively. I would decide upon a
theme. A period of idle thinking would follow where random
scenes, ideas, bits of dialogue, characters, details from dreams
were jotted on bits of paper. These would accumulate into
sequences and a kind of narrative would evolve. This process
was manageable with a short script. However, the feature script
called for a higher level of organisation. The truth was I had no
idea how to write and structure a full-length screenplay. I didn't
know how to tell a story.

I was introduced to the concept of structure through Syd
Field's *The Screenwriter's Workbook*. Initially I was sceptical; it
read like a recipe book. However, with winning simplicity it
spelled out the purest model of structure in the clearest of terms:

Beginning, Middle, End. I looked into other structural models and soon found I began to approach my writing differently. Knowledge of structure gave me all the information I needed to organise and assess my material. It gave me the confidence to experiment with my own structures and rhythms.

Part Two: Punch Drunk

The Work Journal, instigated by the inspirational Les Mills at Newport Film School, encourages a constructive, self-critical approach to everyday, film-making problems. It serves as a useful, ongoing body of reference and information. I will use extracts from these books to illustrate my experience of writing and financing the Welsh feature script *The Kissing Ghost*.

Sept 19 1992, Cardiff

Shame to start on an off note but just months out of Newport and I'm flagging. The script is in trouble. What is the story? A Rites of Passage? A love story? The elements of eco-catastrophe threaten to overwhelm the plot. The surreal elements – incidental music in tap water, moon blowing up etc. have to be integrated and understated if they are going to work. Luca (Villata, friend and business partner) has his own ideas. He reads thirty pages and before he knows it I'm giving him another version of the same thirty pages.

I've been making so many excuses of late – I'm not settled, worried about money. I feel rushed, as if I'm trying to move ahead with the writing without having fully explored the ideas and themes. I owe so much money – about £9000. Luca kindly subbed me some cash against the Italian horse championship promo we're shooting in the spring. I can't face signing on. I'm so caught up with trying to live from week to week I can't think straight.

Nov 6 1992, Poplar

I'm installed at Luca's place in East London. I need a home. He needs someone to look after his place when he's in Italy. Luca is so full of doubts about the project. I can't decide whether his hyper-criticism will spur me on or piss me off.

Nov 28 1992, Poplar

Luca and I argue constantly. I've begun collating ideas for characters and scenes. Luca is obviously frustrated by the impotence of his position. He keeps telling me what the film *must* be – 'easily understood,' 'family entertainment,' 'multi-layered,' 'appealing to investors' and so on. I try to listen and accommodate, if only for appearance's sake. Underneath I feel angry and let down. I want to be left alone to explore the ideas. I won't write this film to order. So many arguments to come....

Feb 3 1993, Poplar
Steve (Gough) rang. He enjoyed KG synopsis. "Great ideas, but couldn't find the dramatic core", where was the "cinematic dynamic"? Luca calls from Turin to say he enjoyed synopsis but where was the "magical angle... spiritual union 'twixt man and planet – otherwise what was film about"? Do I have to sign-post every metaphor, outline every nuance in fucking neon?

Feb 4 1993, Poplar – Birthday
Dreamt of a huge and muscular snake, 40 yards long, making its way along a riverbank. Two kids ran out of a bush and attacked it, skidding down its body, crushing it. Pieces of the snake fell into the river. The snake, once long and elegant, now looked pathetic and wasted. For snake read script.

Feb 13 1993, Poplar – European Script Fund
Finalising our application for £8500 development cash from the Script Fund. Includes a twelve page treatment and detailed development budgets outlining legal fees, office costs, writer's fees, travel expenses and so on. Our total development budget is about £16,000. As the named production company we would be obliged to match the £8000 loan. Once the film was financed the loan becomes repayable with interest. If the film were never made the loan would be written off. Luca and I have each agreed to invest four grand in the project.

April 20 1993, Poplar
Phil Hughes rang from the Script Fund to ask for a show reel. Someone had seen *Dando's Brilliantine* (my graduation film) and recommended it. There's a short-list meeting next week.
May 14 1993, Poplar – Script Fund Interview

With over 1500 scripts applying for cash, we are frankly aston-
ished to have been short-listed. Attended meeting with Christian
Routh and Phil Hughes. Routh told us that when the advisors
initially discussed our application they weren't particularly positive – felt the narrative needed work. Later during lunch the
project came up in conversation and many expressed enthusiasm. The real doubt about our application stems from our lack
of production experience. Luca did well to assure them of our
financial position and business acumen – the fact that he was
(ahem) able to bring in about a third of the budget from private
investors.

June 8 1993, Poplar
Letter from Script Fund. We've got the cash! November deadline for first draft. The money comes in three lumps linked with
the steady progression of the script. The terms of the funding
require us to start a limited company – *Radiant Pictures* (hints
at things toxic as well as things divine). I then have to assign the
rights of *KG* to the company becoming co-owner and co-
producer with Luca.

June 30 1993, Poplar – RCA screening, BAFTA
A neat and terrifying little postscript to the Script Fund cash.
Phil Hughes tells me that *KG* was initially rejected by one of
their readers who failed to see any humour in it. Russ
Gascoigne, a script editor at the BBC, whom I had met for the
first time at the Chapter screening of *Dando*, had rung Phil to
recommend it. Phil dug our treatment out of the bin; the office
read it and 'loved it'. Lucky or what?

July 10 1993, Poplar – Draft one, Day one
Using my treatment as a template I spend the day chipping away
at the first ten pages of Draft One. My days are filled with little
rituals of avoidance: I run little circuits from the computer to the
fridge to the telly. To combat this I decide to build in an exercise
component – if I want to leave the computer I have to carry out
a punishing series of push-ups. Anyway, it's a start.

Sept 9 1993, Poplar
First meeting with script editor Walter Donohue at Faber and Faber. He has worked with Wenders, Potter, and Boorman amongst others. I'd been looking for an editor when I wandered into his master class at the Edinburgh Film Festival. I sent him my treatment, and he said he was interested. I spent a lot of time today explaining the story, the elements, clarifying the writing always with one thing in mind: 'does it say what you want it to say?' He offered suggestions to make the narrative stronger. It's a real pleasure to argue the toss with someone so turned on by film. His conclusion about the current treatment is that it reads too much like a novel. He suggests I strip away the detail and refine the central drama. Put it into outline – without dialogue, assemble the entire film this way then add dialogue. (Why didn't I think of that?)

(From Nov 93 to Dec 94 became involved with writing and directing *Moniker* for BBC Wales' *Wales Playhouse*)

May 18 1994, Cannes
First experience of pitching to producers. Karen Street (Script Fund) is working like a trooper organising meetings for us. The most memorable was this morning's fiasco with Nicole Guillaumette from Sundance. Last night we'd thrown a party on the boat. I'd had a skinful. This morning, Luca and I gingerly shook hands with Nicole on the veranda of the Carlton. We paid the price of a small car for two coffees and a juice and I began my pitch. As I spoke I felt waves of pins and needles in my arms – a sure sign I'm about to be sick. Just as I reached the climax of the story I had to clamp my jaws shut and leg it to a toilet. Luckily, Nicole waited for me to return and finish the story. She was keen. Wants to see the first draft. A quick note about the party last night – some bright spark from the Script Fund threatened to open an umbrella aboard Luca's boat – a big no-no with the superstitious boating fraternity. Luca went white, firmly asked her not to. She wouldn't be told and went ahead. Luca and Michaelangelo blew a gasket. The party now over, Luca bitterly explained, "We haven't worked off the bad luck from the last umbrella yet...."

May 29 1994, Cardiff – Wales Film Council

We'd applied to the WFC for £10,000 development money. We arrived at the meeting confident, very happy to get support from Wales. We left looking like we'd been smacked in the face. The administrators spent the whole meeting picking holes in our project – why did we have a lawyer? Why start a production company? "This is big boys stuff, this would not do at all". I calmly explained that we had simply carried out the terms set down by the Script Fund and, considering their level of support, we thought them entirely reasonable. "Well you shouldn't have gone to the Script Fund!" They treated Luca and I like a couple of naughty boys. On the way out Luca is deciding how to word where he would like them to stick their money. I see his point though I would prefer to work with them than without them. After all, this is the only Welsh input we have.

July 20 1994, Poplar – Draft One Final Day

I can remember saying those words to Nicole at Cannes, "Two weeks, we can send you the first draft in two weeks". Two months later, here I am gazing tenderly at ninety-four pages of what-I-would-describe-as-linear-but-others-might-disagree-type-narrative. And a sexy little wad it is too.

April 3 1995. Poplar – Draft Three

I am losing my mind. The Script Fund deadline has come and gone. Can hear suspicion creeping into the voice of the woman from Contracts who needs the new script and our accounts pronto. I cannot work because of a long tale of woe with word processor. It started some time ago. The Amstrad started to crash when I pressed the shift key. So, I wrote in lower case. I would then press the shift key without thinking, sending tens of pages of brand new script into oblivion. Already borrowed more money than was polite from Dad and Luca. Arrange overdraft extension and buy a second hand IBM 486. Eventually get going with 'new' machine. Weeks later, in full flow on third draft, the 486 breaks down. I ring the bloke from Newport who sold it to me. He was unrepentant, cheerful even, "corrupted hard disk ... could happen anytime ... fix it for cost ... you hadn't backed up your files ... hope there was nothing valuable on it!'". Ring bank to arrange extension on the extension to pay for repairs. Call computer repairman. Make appointment. The woman from Contracts calls again, "Is there a reason for your non-compliance with the contract...." I promise to personally deliver everything she needs in two days. Computer repairman doesn't show. He phones to apologise and makes new appointment for six p.m. He doesn't show. At seven he rings with an appointment for the following day. Computer man goes on to miss six appointments over two days. I live in fear of the phone ringing. Luca in Italy. Feel like I'm taking on too much.

April 19 1995, Poplar
Script Fund report on Draft Three very positive: 'potential cult hit', 'extraordinary', 'original' etc.

(Richard Staniforth becomes *KG* Producer)

Sept 22 1995, Berlin Rendezvous
Rendezvous is a Euro Aim initiative. Radiant pays £3800 to attend a three-day pitching session at the Hilton, a flash hotel/shopping mall in East Berlin. Our fee buys us 15 meetings with potential financiers and distributors. Richard and I wade through a daunting but encouraging schedule – ten extra meetings were requested by various financiers. General response to *KG* was excellent. About eight seriously interested parties, Leslie Porter (CIBY 2000) and Susan Minas (Alliance Films) amongst the most enthusiastic. It's thrilling. Richard and I are striding these soulless corridors like we belong. Richard says I tell a different story when I pitch to women than when I pitch to men. With women it's all emotion, desire and need. With men it's plot, mechanics and special effects.

Oct 9 1995 Llanfrynach, Brecon
Finally haul my sorry, cityworn arse out of London into a rural wet dream. Greeted by a letter from Simon Perry of British Screen. He found *KG* "too confusing, too complicated to persevere with..." I think he 'persevered' as far as page nine. It's Bad News to file with the rest. Richard tried to be upbeat but I know he worries about the perceived difficulty of the script.

Oct 25 1995, Cardiff
One month after Rendezvous and all is quiet. Glum.

Jan 26 1996, Cardiff
Had a fax from Susan Minas of Alliance in Toronto – reader's script report of *KG*. First page peppered with compliments. Next two pages – a pretty thorough demolition of script – too encoded, too personal, main character Arthur too awkward to be likeable.

Feb 21 1996, Intercity 125
Brushing aside a pile of rejection letters from Rendezvous contacts, Richard and I arrive at Film on Four for a meeting with Kate Leys, development officer. She is very keen indeed, loves script – "phenomenal piece of writing". Suggests we go away and put together a team and a package. I can barely believe it. Karen Street can't believe it either. Tells me not to expect too much from C4. They don't like first time directors.

Mar 12 1996, Cardiff
Draft Four submitted to Channel 4. I'm glad to be free of it once again. The endless revisions. Returning again and again to pieces of dialogue, replaying scenes in my head like a bad case of delirium. My partner says it's like living with a zombie. I am so obsessive of late, closed off. My moods are slowly but surely grinding her down and I've got no answers for her.

April 11 1996. Bordeaux – Equinoxe '96
The Script Fund put *KG* forward to Equinoxe Script Lab, an all- expenses paid week in Bordeaux funded by Sony and Canal Plus. *KG* is in good company. Scripts from seven screenwriters from all over the world. Most notably from my viewpoint American Lodge Kerrigan (*Clean Shaven*) and Australian Rolf De Heer (*Bad Boy Bubby*). Industry 'consultants' are invited to work on the assembled scripts. Among them the superb Jacques Audiard (director), David Giler (producer of *Alien*), Duncan Thompson and Don Macpherson. Endless food, vintage wines from the vines of Chateau Beychevelle, and a whole week having my script torn to shreds. It's bloody great. The response

to *KG* ranged from "best script I've read in ten years" to complete incomprehension from a Sicilian whom, upon hearing that I was from Wales, enquired if I'd seen *The Englishman Who Went Up A Hill, But Came Down A Mountain.* "Very humorous, very pure". This week has been an incredibly positive experience. As much a psychological boost as anything else. Why couldn't we organise something like this back home?

July 19 1996, Cardiff
Letter from Kate Leys (Film on Four) apologising for being out of touch. She doesn't think script is ready for production – partly because she feels I am not ready to direct my first feature. Get giddy. Swallow hard. Blood boils. True I don't have a huge track record – a couple of half-hour dramas for telly including a networked BBC Wales Playhouse. I know our 'package' is strong – Miranda Richardson and Anthony Hopkins as principals, Dante Spinotti (*Heat* and *Nell*) to shoot. Four years of toiling on this project, only to be told I am the perceived weak link.

Dec 29 1996, Cardiff – C4
Invited to lunch with Kate Leys. I rang to refuse. Didn't see the point of meeting if it were for consolation's sake. The secretary was adamant. It was a 'working meeting'. Richard's option on *KG* has run out. We're looking for another producer. I go alone to C4. The meeting was very positive. Seems there's more money for Film on Four this year. Reading between the lines they are probably looking for projects to resurrect. I promise showreels and latest draft. On we go.

Jan 10 1997, Cardiff
Michelle Ryan of Teliesyn is our new producer. Michelle sees *KG* as having to work on its own terms, as a 'unique vision', or not at all. Draft Five is focused, characters are integrated, emotion comes off the page.

Aug 11 1997, Cardiff
Unbelievably, after all the assurances and guarantees of regular communication from Kate at Film on Four, we have not received one word from her office since December, despite

bombarding them with every form of human correspondence, short of ransom notes written in blood.

June 12 1999, Nant Gwrtheyrn

Michele and I are enrolled on the Arista 'story-editing' course with the *Kissing Ghost*. It has been an intense five days working to unlock the 'emotional core' of the script. Hannah Kodicek is our advisor. An aficionado of hard-core Russian fairy stories, she connected well with *KG*. At our final advisory meeting this morning, as we talked our way through the story, I swear there were tears. Now beginning sixth draft of *Kissing Ghost*.

ADDENDUM – Nov 1999

It has been an encouraging year for the Welsh 'hijra.' Peter Edwards' *Nuts and Bolts* is shot entirely in Merthyr Tydfil and uses Welsh accents, actors, writers and directors to create a groundbreaking home grown 'soap.' Hard on its heels is the BBC Wales drama series *Bryn-Coed*.

The revamped PICS, now called Welsh Rarebits goes from strength to strength. Meanwhile, Big Little Pictures – a Sgrîn/HTV initiative aims to create two half-hour dramas for cinema, year on year. The first couple of films will be premiered at the Welsh International Film Festival, with a further two projects announced for production in Y2K. And let's not forget the prestigious DM Davies Award; still the largest cash/services prize for a short film in Europe.

There *is* more cause for optimism; but this is no time for complacency, for jumping on the Cool Cymru pop bandwagon. We need to lay down infrastructures to secure public or private finance; we need to organise training and nurture new writers, producers, directors. And as we set up office and plan our way forward, as we agonise over whether to opt for the Hollywood-style producer-led studio system, or the auteur-driven, state-subsidised European model, we should not lose sight of the fact that cinema is a province illuminated by the random brilliance of unstoppable zealots with a Big Idea. And you can't regulate for that.

Making House of America:
An Interview with Marc Evans and Ed Thomas

Eventually released in the UK in September 1997, *House of America* and the story of its making are central to any account of an emerging Welsh film industry. Two of the creative talents behind it, Marc Evans, the director and Ed Thomas, the writer have come to be seen as two of the voices with a realistic chance of achieving the kind of international recognition that contemporary Welsh culture craves.

The interview they kindly gave was at the point when *House of America* had been completed and shown in various, limited ways, but had not had a full cinema release.

It is included here not simply as an account of a key film, but also as a story of what is to be celebrated about trying to make films within contemporary Welsh culture alongside the aspects that make it so hard. There are accounts here of the practicalities of getting funding, of the attitudes of broadcasters, of Wales in relation to Scotland, and of their own personal influences as well as detailed discussion of key aesthetic decisions about *House of America* itself. In all it adds up to a fascinating and personal tale of independent film-making today, powerfully inflected with what it means to try and root your work in Wales.

Since the interview was completed *House of America* has had mixed fortunes. Its distribution was limited after the promising London opening at several prominent art houses and its eventual box office record was extremely disappointing to everyone involved. Critically though it fared better; a number of the main broadsheets had very positive things to say about it filmically and a number "got the joke" to use Ed Thomas' own phrase. The critical 'establishment' in the shape of *Sight and Sound* seemed to miss the point and take issue with it as a failed issue-based film rather than see it on its own terms.

There was in the end, though, enough interested reaction

both inside and outside Wales for both Evans and Thomas to progress to more relatively high profile projects: Evans' *Resurrection Man* was considered a powerful and original variation on the usual filmic treatments of the Irish conflict and Thomas has not only had further success as a theatre writer but has made his first feature as a director, a film based on James Hawes novel, *Rancid Aluminium.*

SB: Can we start by talking about the process of getting *House of America* made?
ET: It took along time to get the money together. We first took it to television in about 1989. People like Michael Waring [at BBC Drama in London] and Estelle Daniel. They very much wanted to make a realistic thing about incest and unemployment, issue-based drama. I thought it was a real turkey myself; I didn't know anything about screenplays. And it just died a death in the end. That was the first draft.

It took another four years to start again. Marc did *Thicker Than Water* with Sheryl Crown as a producer at BBC Wales and she asked what he wanted to do next and he was really keen on *House* so she gave some of the money from *Thicker Than Water* to develop the screenplay. The next draft was done for a small amount of that money.
ME: Because we didn't know anything about raising money for a feature and as the story is set in South Wales it seemed completely logical at the time to approach the Welsh-based TV companies for the money. We found out pretty quickly to be honest that neither the money nor the will was here to make *House.* Had there been a bit more will then they would probably have found the money to make it as a taped studio piece or TV drama. It kind of went into abeyance for a while. It became this project that nobody would be interested in. We did have this image problem for trying to raise money in London; it became this grim story about drug taking and incest in the regions really, as they thought of it. Then something changed, and what changed really was meeting with British Screen. They thought the script needed work on it and they were wary that all my experience so far was in television which was a bit of a dirty word for them because they are about encouraging new film

directors. But Steve Cleary who we worked with there was probably the biggest supporter of the script from beginning to end. We were protesting too much really – we were so aware of the negative image of a social realist piece that the first thing he said to us was, "You've got to stop explaining the joke boys. I get the joke." When he said "I get the joke" we felt this huge sense of relief. He helped us get the script into a form whereby his immediate superior, Simon Perry, would believe in it and like it. He made us aware of things we didn't know we had to do. For example we didn't know we had to write director's notes. Like a kind of manifesto of what kind of film it was going to be. And he was very good at getting me to understand how I wanted to do this. One example he used was when Andrew Birkin was trying to get money for *Cement Garden* he put into his director's notes that the colour of Charlotte Gainsbourg's bikini would become a more lurid shade of green during the film; it's a clever thing to do, it kind of wets somebody's appetite not just for the film but for the kinds of pictures and images that you are going to make.

ET: He [Steve Cleary] was the first to say that he got the joke and that he understood what we meant when we said that it was a celebration not a miserabilist film. It made us all relax because for five years we'd had these conversations about what kind of film it was going to be. It was a big liberation. He used to come to script meetings with no notes and he'd say "Page 75, Boyo's line," and he'd paraphrase the line, "I don't know if you need that". There's a sliding scale into tragedy down the back end and he suggested that. He understood the script didn't he? It gives you confidence when somebody hasn't got a Robert McKee book on story structure on his right hand side, a huge wad of notes on the other and your script in the middle talking script edit rubbish really. He was really cool about it. Also he said that the script should be less than a hundred pages and it was a hundred and twenty in the final draft. He just said I know a font that if you cut the descriptions in half will bring it down to ninety-nine! And he was right – it came to ninety-eight and a half! It sounds really glib, but he said that people want a read that is a hundred pages. So he knows the business and also when he talked to Marc, knew the ideas behind making a romantic film about unemployment, incest and drug taking.

SB: At this point then did British Screen talk to other backers?

ME: Once you get British Screen on board, the producer Sheryl Crown had to work very hard then. They would only give, I think, a third of the budget, but they were on our side and they are very good at politics. Simon Perry for example then suggested that we got the next tranche, as they call it, of money from Holland. They had helped the Dutch Film Board out with *Antonia's Line* the year before. They had tried to work initially on the basis of co-production, they'd found ultimately that it was going to be a Dutch film with a Dutch cast and very much the film that the Dutch wanted to make. So they said to them we'll give you the money to help you make the film and you can help make one of our films.

ET: What was good about British Screen was that the Dutch gave them a choice of which film to back and they were expecting a choice in return of about three or four different films and British Screen said *House* or nothing.

ME: That was very supportive, because in a way what the Dutch were hoping for in return, quite understandably, was that British Screen would get them involved in something which wasn't difficult. And of course British Screen used the favour to get the money for something which otherwise would have been difficult to raise extra money for. So we went ahead with British Screen plus Dutch money. At that time, because we knew that there were some sections that we wanted to shoot in America we thought that maybe we could get Canadian money, so it was becoming quite complicated and slow. There was a re-organisation in Canadian film financing and they fell out so we ended up getting some money from First Independent as distributors who are attached to HTV and the branch of HTV called Harvest I think. It was basically television money which is why we really stitched ourselves up a bit by committing to a television broadcast 'regionally' for a film that we tried so hard to make a cinema film. This was a point of principle which I think in retrospect we feel a bit sorry that we lost. Even if we'd known at the time we'd probably still have gone for it because we needed the money.

ET: But it was a small amount of money. With the glorious vision of hindsight you'd think we shouldn't have done that, but it's still a low-budget film and we needed the money. I think Menna in HTV and Geraint Morris are big fans of the film and it was just internal politics that prompted its showing on the box before Christmas.

SB: Do you know what kind of size TV audience it got?

ET: I think we got away with it actually. First Independent thought it was no problem because it's 'only Wales' at the end of the day. But from our point of view, because it's such a cinematic film ... all films should eventually be seen on the TV: it's not a snob thing, but in Wales often people who commission things don't know the difference between cinema and TV. There is a fundamental difference; this is a cinema film in its concept so it's disappointing that the first time people in Wales saw it outside a premiere was on the telly on a small screen. And for him as a director more than me as a writer it's just not the best way to launch a film. But it puts into context just how difficult it is for people like Endaf Emlyn; *Y Mapiwr* and *Gadael Lenin* got a such limited distribution ... and for all that effort to get just one screening on the box and that's it. Marc's film *Ymadawiad Arthur* went out on Boxing Day, it only had one S4C screening – it was funded through the light entertainment budget rather than drama – but after one screening that's it. No cinema distribution.

ME: No life really.

ET: If you were out on Boxing Day your Gran's going to say what the fuck's this! It's in black and white, it's all about people with fucking funny heads walking through the universe and talking funny Welsh, set in the future! It's all about getting the language of television right and the language of film right and knowing what the difference is.

ME: At this stage what saved us really was the Lottery coming in and giving us the money to finish it [*House*]. It's a very strange feeling in a way because part of you really regrets the politics that has created the situation where the Lottery is so important yet to be honest we have benefited from it. The kind of journey that we have taken in a way ... my first film was funded, only ten thousand quid in total, by the Welsh Arts Council, my first crack at making something outside television as an independent film, and then over ten years later the people that allow your film to be made are the Lottery and I suppose that's the difference. There's a real story there in how films get made now.

ET: We went through a period of time ... it was a 'despite' thing. I remember sitting in a pub with you and being really happy because there was no Welsh money in it!

ME: It would have been really interesting to make an independent Welsh feature film, the first one for ages, without any Welsh money! We almost felt gleeful at the prospect when it looked like we might get all the money from outside Wales. It's perverse, but almost to prove a point.... In the end it was a real lesson in how to raise money, but also it was a messy thing and though I'm really glad that *House of America* is perceived as a Welsh film, in my heart I know it's a Welsh film almost by default.

ET: We don't really want to be part of a complaint culture either. We went through a stage when things looked really black, February about three or four years ago, when we just decided not to be pessimistic. Wales has got a healthy 'despite culture', things happen despite what goes on. Bands, everything else. But I'm really keen for this piece not to sound like a complaint. I'd hate this thing to just be about 'We made it anyway and two fingers up to the establishment', all countries have establishments and the economics of the culture of Wales is not going to be promoted by having competitive animals, BBC, S4C and HTV fight against each other. It needs a vision, even if it's only for two or three years. Glasgow was re-made – *Glasgow's Miles Better* was made by a £6 million investment from the Mayor of Glasgow. I would argue that it needs the same cohesion and vision here. But it's not up to us – we're just the makers, not the businessmen. But it's something to do with the vision thing. Having a vision and investing wisely into something which the press are calling this Welsh explosion in pop or whatever else. It's not an explosion, because there's no infrastructure to sustain it. Ours is a 'despite film' I reckon. But not a 'complaint despite film'. If Wales had wanted to invest in it, it would have been much easier. But hopefully it's a better film now because we are now four years better at writing and directing.

ME: To be honest, in the context of Wales a certain amount of fatigue sets in. Because you say to yourself, nobody wants me to make this film or even other films. But you have to realise in the end that this is not necessarily a Welsh phenomenon.

When you're in your twenties it's like you're knocking on the door of your culture and maybe complaining that your culture doesn't give you what you want, by the time you get to your thirties you think that perhaps you should be contributing to the culture, not complaining about what it's not giving you. You have to find some kind of strategy, which ended up being some kind of quite messy one with *House*, of grabbing a piece of money or support for something you want to get made. I think Ed had more experience of those kinds of battles from having to do it through theatre, albeit the amount of money being less, you're still dealing with organisations that you have to galvanise into giving you money. It's a difficult area to be in because you're straddling commerce and art; you're trying to motivate people who are interested in original voices from Wales, but also, in any industry a million quid is a lot of money. When I made my first Arts Council film, *Johnny Be Good* for ten thousand quid I felt a lot of responsibility, but when it gets to £1.3 million that really is a lot. You don't get it that easily. When you've got it and you've made your film you become more philosophical about it, but in a small country it's not that easy. But at the same time you regret a bit that there wasn't at least a bit more will.

ET: The very first bit of feedback I got when *House* was a stage play was when a man from S4C came to see it and his flippant response was that it was very good and all that, but nobody from west Wales would know who Jack Kerouac was. And that was it ... wiped out the screenplay. I genuinely thought, well, that's fair enough bla, bla, bla.... But looking back it's such a flippant remark. It fundamentally loses the plot. It comes back to vision again. There was a time when I would cheerfully have spat over every broadcaster in Wales but not now. The 'despite culture' is a kind of celebration.

SB: *House* is already being bracketed together with *Twin*

Town as part of something new in Wales that has a relationship in turn to *Trainspotting et al.* How far are you happy to go along with this?

ME: There're things happening and it's often difficult to know whether it's coincidence or what. At the time when we started to get the support of British Screen there seemed to be more interest around and more sources of money starting to appear for films that were sort of representing forgotten regions if you like. An exact contemporary of mine, Michael Winterbottom's first film *Butterfly Kiss* was made by British Screen for very little money and it was shot on the motorways of the north of England and then you get Scottish films coming out. I'm really not interested at all in the *Trainspotting* comparison, but it's quite interesting to look at the kind of films that have surprised people lately and at films that have been people's first features – *Boston Kickout* is another one, they aren't swinging London films.

ET: More like back of beyond films!

ME: And the second thing I've found very interesting is that at the moment when we felt most frustrated by our desire to make something in Wales we were working in other areas, like Crw Byw and now a few years on TV is seen as the opposition, a threat to a real film culture. But I've got this theory that in Wales what happened with S4C in particular meant that TV had a different relationship to the culture than it had in other countries. It was like the cultural equivalent to the argument for nuclear armament; Pakistan saying we have to have a nuclear bomb, because everyone else has one, but the question is do we really need one. In cultural terms a lot of people would say that the Welsh language doesn't need television, it is what it is and what is embodied in it, it doesn't need television to legitimise it, but because everyone else has television you can't, as it were, culturally disarm unilaterally! You have to have television. So once we had television we didn't know quite what to do with it. It was essential to have it, but it created this strange and interesting relationship with the culture. For example with music we were operating a model that doesn't exist anywhere else in Britain or even in Europe: people knew there were bands out there, so you had to have a youth programme to represent the bands, but

S4C was paying for the bands to be recorded and someone like me to come in and make a pop promo for that band which was then put into a show which really represented a lie, if you like: that we actually had a pop industry, but it was one made up by the television industry.

Five or six years later the person making the video, me, is making a feature film and the people who were in those bands are now Catatonia and Super Furry Animals.

So lately I feel a great affection for the early mechanics of the relationship between telly and culture. We started creating a culture, sort of in our own backyard because by definition the Welsh language products don't naturally have such a wide audience as things in the English language. Eventually some of us started making things in English, not because we didn't want to work in Welsh. We kind of came up through a system which was at times frustrating because it didn't give us the chance to make our film, but it did allow us to have a crack at a visual/musical media in a way which we would never have had in England because the relationship just didn't exist there.

ET: In the same way if you look at *Pobol Y Cwm* – it's only a boom shadow away from being a beautiful absurdist drama. It creates a fantasy that there's a Welsh language audience, that gynaecologists speak in Welsh to hookers in Carmarthen. It's a fantastically absurd idea, but if it's treated properly, with style, it's a brilliant idea because you can have the same acting style, drop the boom in and show it's fiction. When people leave the Deri Arms have them walk into a TV studio. You can actually say that Wales exists in a TV studio. That's what I mean by this vision thing; if you just slightly tilt it we have a beautifully diverse and interesting culture which can be recorded and produced on television. But S4C's remit was to have a broad base and they bought and copied a lot of programmes; you had *Blind Date* etc in Welsh. I accept the fact that it had to be a broad audience, but what's brilliant I think is that it's created people that can look at the interesting possibilities of a Welsh language soap in a country that doesn't exist. However you look at Wales it doesn't exist as a country. A country is a territory governed by its own people, and we aren't. It's an imagined nation and if it's imagined then the television culture, whilst still making sheepdog trials and quiz shows, could have a style that was just on a tilt, still with beautiful soap opera that works for ninety percent of the people but with no exteriors. Wales really does exist in a TV studio. This is really interesting if you can control the frame; what Wales has failed to do I think is control the frame. There's still the possibility though. We know that we cannot sell fifty minute TV dramas abroad if they are in Welsh, but we can sell cinema films, and one of the things again with the glorious vision of hindsight is that we could have had a structure similar to David Rose's Film on Four. It's starting to happen now with some of the BBC and S4C's ideas on distribution, but it's twelve or thirteen years behind.

ME: It's full of contradictions though in a way, because I have to say that I can't imagine anybody except S4C giving me money to make a black and white science-fiction film on super-16 and blowing it up to 35mm just for festival release. You wouldn't be allowed to make that kind of film for the BBC so there're certain advantages to not always being that commercial and set in your ways. What you learn is that you have to look for those pockets of money and start influencing things that way.

ET: I would argue again that that's the 'despite culture', because you can see the gaps in it. But the thing is, we might also see the gaps in a proper pyramid structure as well. The lack of that vision to have proper structure means that we are still trying to do it now. All broadcasting companies will have gaps, but in Wales we have a culture, a film industry, a music industry based on default not on strategy. And I would say that it would be better with a strategy – still look for the gaps because the wrong people get the jobs anyway. But I want to belong to a culture in Wales which has a visible strategy to outsiders. There will always be gaps because it comes down to us versus the establishment. *House of America* would be a difficult film for any cultural establishment, Wales is no different in that. But for years we were internationally a laughing stock because we had no strategy for films. For the likes of us it would mean that we would be faster on our feet, I think, if the strategy was in place and visible to an international market.

SB: Do you think any kind of strategy is now going to emerge on the back of the 'accidents'?

ET: Maybe.

ME: There's a lot of bullshit spoken about TV versus film. But one of the reasons that I think film is so important is that it's an area where you can still foster an idea of independence. What's been lacking in Wales is the infrastructure to foster independent film-making, even if it's just the perception of independence. A sum of money that's kept apart. It doesn't matter if it comes from the broadcasters, the lottery or whoever, so long as the job is seen as a long term investment. We are lucky now in that our first film is perceived to be interesting and has got a bit of attention, but it could be that somebody has to take the risk that a first film is not necessarily going to be that brilliant. You have to be looking at the third and fourth film.

ET: In the end it's the voice that's important. Making a script into 3-D in collaboration with actors and cinematographers etc., but with a unique voice. It's not like television, you have to be able to 'see' and that's the hardest thing to define. Who can tell when somebody walks into the door whether they can see or not? In a way it is an argument for unadulterated art. Fictions are lies that tell the truth. Michael Billington is always arguing that playwrights should write about issues relevant to contemporary Britain. I'd prefer to discuss those in the pub. Fiction is life imagined not life reproduced. We are paid to imagine. He's paid to imagine in 3-D, I'm paid to imagine in words. It's life imagined not reproduced. It's much better to reproduce through journalism. Sometimes fictional forms get close to the truth, but it's achieved by the biggest lie. This is something that people are still fundamentally afraid of.

SB: Bringing this idea of a 'unique voice' a bit closer to home, how do you see a 'Marc Evans film'?

ET: Marc's a bloke who involves the scriptwriter more than anything. When we were going to the Sundance festival he said to us "Look boys I'm going to get all the credit here, it's a director's festival," and I feel completely at home with that. It's a directors medium. But with Marc I always felt like I knew how he was going to shoot it because we had worked together so much on the script. I only turned up for about five days on the set because I had nothing to do. I had complete confidence that I knew how he was going to do it. I would never become a screenwriter in the ordinary sense because it's completely disempowering. But with Marc it was partly to do with a journey of friendship, sharing the same thing, not having defined roles and Marc does the same with the art department and the actors.

SB: Can we just pick up on the involvement of the French cinematography team? How did you get them involved?

ME: The way it came about was through the fact that we ended up with a co-production and the Dutch thought that we should have a Dutch cinematographer. To be honest my first reaction was to go for broke – Robbie Muller who shot all Jim Jarmush's films. I asked if he was available and they said no we couldn't afford Robbie Muller and they sent me one tape of a cinematographer, Marc something or other. I thought if someone came to Wales and wanted a Welsh cinematographer I could think of at least three tapes I could send them and at least there would be some choice. I felt a bit that my film was already being taken away from me. So I made a case for saying that it was important to have a cinematographer who was going to help me learn and all those sorts of arguments, not just have someone coming in just because it was a co-production. There was also the credibility thing, I hadn't made a feature film before, but I knew I wanted to make the film in a certain way, so I was trying to quote films that I liked. They were often films that looked liked they would go a certain way, but which had been lifted by the poetry of the cinematographer. One of the films that I quoted was *La Haine*. As a script it could have been thought of as *House* was originally – a little bit grim and a little bit miserable, but I just thought it was a wonderfully poetic film in which the cinematography, the operating as well as the lighting I have to say, created that world. It's a fable really about three boys, a Jew, an Arab, and a black guy going to the palace for the night. I thought it was a wonderful film. All credit to Sheryl, our producer, she said why don't you go for them. It was then much easier to fight my corner with the Dutch by saying 'Why don't you use this person?' they couldn't gainsay that. So I wrote a fax to Pierre and George introducing myself and the whole concept of

Banwen and Ed Thomas etc. etc. They came over and we met them and I knew straight away that I would like to work with them. I didn't really know what to expect; I was expecting people with ponytails and mobile phones, but they were very down to earth and interested in ideas rather than what they could get out of it. I then went over to spend a weekend with them. It was a kind of courtship I suppose. I was really glad when they finally came over that I had gone with them, because apart from the fact that they were really stimulating to work with, they came and looked at our landscape, our place, with the eyes of people that are not from here. Sometimes you can maybe have this problem of trying to get credibility for your project by having an international flavour and end with a hotch potch or Euro-pudding. But by just having this one element that was different it worked really well.

ET: They thought the grass was black. Is it true to say that the bleach by-pass idea came from them saying the grass was black.

ME: They were very interested in the idea that you could see the coal beneath the grass. And the whole thing of ideas leading to pictures. There's a strong visual structure to *House* which is to do with the relationships in the family. One example of the way they work is when we were deciding which format we were going to shoot it on: I wanted to go for the widest format and they said "Why?" and I said because it's the widest and I want to make a feature film, and they said you need to look at what you want to put in your frame; if there are three people in your frame then the widest is the most interesting, but if you are going to do a lot of singles then a squarer format is better because there will be more close-ups and of course *House* is about three kids. They were always asking things of me which helped me define how I was going to shoot my film.

ET: They also always wanted to work from the script out which is not a usual way to work. People tend to think it's image, but the image works from the script into 3-D then into how the camera structure works. Marc could then work with Tiger Tildsley in the art department and together with Pierre and George you would have everyone in three key departments talking the same language before anyone walked on set. That's a fictional language, not a language about how to present gritty hopeless Banwen that's not even on the map. In the end the wide format was right, because *House of America* complains about the lack of a Welsh mythology compared to the American dream; if you can show this in a context which is wide and big and then show America small and in black and white ... it's one of the biggest cheats of all I think. No-one has ever come out and said that in the film Wales looks wide and big while America looks small and black and white. That's the complete double con. It starts with script, but it developed through this collaboration into 3-D, a collaboration of lies to get at the truth. We got a terrible review in *Variety*, you and me were slaughtered for being heightened terrible poets right? But they all thought that this was what Wales was like. There were pinks and yellows and a Norman Bates house and they though it was meant to be gritty realism à la Ken Loach or Mike Leigh. He was fucking thrilled! We'd gone so far away from realism, to think that someone had thought it was real was a real compliment.

ME: There's no cars in the streets.

ET: It's wildly fucking romantic really. Everything is calculated and thought through and I think it's a great compliment that American *Variety* end up thinking that we're just a bunch of white trash trying to make a piece of realism! Because we know that they could not be further from the truth.

SB: Can you talk a bit about the thinking behind the casting of *House*?

ET: If we'd done it in '89 all the original cast of the stage play would have been right. Rich [Lynch] was 23, Russell Gomer was 29. It's then really difficult to explain to actors who are also your friends that they are no longer part of the frame because it's not that fiction any more. If you say *House of America* to Rich or Russ, Russ particularly, he thinks that it's the same performance, but through Marc and the other collaborators it's become a film based on a play, but it's not the play, there are fundamental differences.

ME: Just in practical terms the strategy for the casting was originally to cast as many Welsh actors as possible, partly because the vernacular is so Welsh. In the end we did break the rule by casting Steve Mackintosh as Sid. In order to try and be even handed and also to fight off any possibilities of 'name' actors being foisted on us.

ET: Angelica Huston playing Mam!

ME: There was the inevitable pressure to get name actors in, so what I suggested we should do was offer the opportunity to any actor that we were potentially interested in, and there were not many who were not Welsh, to come and do readings with other actors to try and build up this family. When I first saw the play it knocked my socks off to be honest, so in a way it was extremely important to get away from the original cast and a second practical thing was that the cast of the stage play had all become older and really in film the cast had to be the age of the characters. Having said that you have to work from the people who are around and it's not just about age. We did these open auditions and a lot of Welsh actors became involved; it was a very difficult decision in the end. Steve Mackintosh came in and gave us a *version* of Sid that was just right for the film. If you pushed me to define that, it was that Russ Gomer's original stage version, which I loved, showed us the impossibility of this character achieving anything like his dreams. When it came to the film you've got a man on a motorbike seen through a long lens and you have to at least consider the idea that the person is going to become immediately heroic. You have to play a different game on film. And because you are going to have an audience that may know nothing of what it is to be Welsh, you have to have someone who when they get on that bike has the possibility of looking heroic. We had pangs of Welsh non-conformist guilt about it because we really thought that we were in a position to cast it completely Welsh, but at the end of the day you have to keep your mind open and his accent and atti-tude were just right for the Sid character in the film. In a way it's quite ironic that the one 'outsider' that we cast is also the outsider in the film. The film also changed during casting; to be honest my original idea was to find a Gwenny who was sixteen. I did all sorts of open auditions. I went to schools, but the thing I've learnt about casting is that you can't just invent a sixteen-year old girl capable of playing what is quite a difficult part so in the end Lisa Palfrey came in and we made Gwenny older and Boyo younger, and in a way all that was for the good, because it helped the film to get further and further away from the play and it becomes a different story. Boyo is the young one and Gwenny and Sid get closer in age. This gives you a different version of incest. By degrees the film became a different version. There is a point at which an adapted film has to start defining itself, to separate it from the original work and casting is one of the things that help this to happen. The strategy for the casting was in the end very good. I didn't make it a battle between producers wanting 'names' in and us wanting only Welsh people. Everybody who was interested I said to them don't sit there and try and do a Welsh accent; I put non-Welsh actors with Welsh actors and inexperienced actors with experienced ones and then I'd swap them around a few times. I said I don't want to practice directing, just take you through reading a few scenes from the script. I think everybody who did it felt that they had a good crack at it and that it was part of a search for a genuine new version.

SB: So there was no pressure on the casting process?

ME: Initially there was some to get names in. But Ed and I adopted a kind of bargaining strategy and said from the start that the only part that was negotiable was Mam. The kids just have to be able to sell this idea of them being kids that have never been anywhere. Mam can be a little bit different. But when somebody starts talking to you about 'courting' and all that that involves some American star who might be prepared to slum it a bit and get into a Welsh film you realised that you could not take the risk. If she appeared in any way American it would just devalue the whole story. That really reduced it to British people and in a way we won our argument for getting the people we wanted by stealth. In the end, on our budget the pressure wasn't that great to go for names, but it is now perhaps slightly more difficult to get the film distributed widely because it hasn't got Susan Sarandon in it, nevertheless I'd rather have that problem than have compromised earlier and had someone play a part that wasn't really appropriate for them.

SB: What kind of distribution deal have you ended up with?

ET: First Independent are doing it. It's a tough sell you know. When the film had first been cut we were cock-a-hoop, but then we went through a trough because the film was shown in Milan and none of the American distributors bought it. They didn't say they didn't want to buy it, but none of them jumped straight in; they were all like lemmings round a pool and if one of them had gone for it they would probably all have followed. I remember Sheryl Crown coming back hugely disappointed, because they wanted a hit, a money hit, but at the same time knowing that the film was conceived as an arthouse release. There were lots of factors involved; it wasn't handled very well at Sundance. We had the competition of *Twin Town* with the cast and crew all being flown over there first class, a huge publicity budget. There was just us with no leaflets, posters or anything. The publicist thought that Sean Connery was Welsh and Anthony Hopkins was Scottish. But at the end of the day *House* is still the film that we wanted to make and if people had told us beforehand that it was going to open in the Screen on the Green in September and The Ritzy in Brixton and The Rio, Dalston and Chapter Arts Centre then that was exactly what we intended to do. It's decent distribution at the end of the day; five or six cinemas in the West End and if it works, their strategy comes from that. It's more of a slow dribble rather than opening in multiplexes for a week and dying a death because it doesn't make the box office. It's what we always intended and with any luck and some good reviews this way it will have two or three months in the public eye.

ME: We have to remember that it's still low-budget and it's still a first feature and it's got no stars in it in box-office terms. We felt really happy that we managed to achieve as much as we have in the time. For some people there has been a feeling of disappointment that it hasn't suddenly been snapped up, especially by American distributors.

ET: That might still happen after a British release. It happened like that with *Trainspotting* for example. That started off as a really good novel which turned into a really good play and then into a really good film, but became a phenomenon by default.

ME: You have got a slight practical problem in that if some-body invests a small amount of money in the film then they don't have to do that much to protect their investment. So what you really need, which *Trainspotting* did get eventually, is some-body protecting their investment by putting a lot of money into publicity. It's not vanity comparing *House* to *Trainspotting,* it's just that it's a Scottish film on a similar scale. Nobody is going to put a lot of money into publicising *House* realistically so there is only one strategy and that is to get some decent audiences and reviews from distribution in key cinemas at a time when there aren't a lot of other films around.

SB: Is that the reason for the delay until September?

ME: That's right. The summer's terrible; it's all big films for kids. Adults don't tend to go to the cinema. There're a lot of students around in September for example.

ET: Also *House* won't survive in the market without carefully finding a niche for it, because it's a certain kind of film. *The English Patient* plays in arthouses and multiplexes. There's no longer a sacrosanct rule whereby one film plays Chapter and another plays the Odeon. But there's huge competition. There were a hundred and forty films made in Britain last year; at least thirty have got to be half tidy. For the Capital Odeon in Cardiff it's more lucrative to play *101 Dalmatians* for an extra week than to show *House*. So it needs very careful nurturing. There's also luck. They'll try and place it in a week that's quiet, that's part of the strategy, but it will need good reviews in the ABC news-papers. Then maybe *The Mirror* or *The Sun* will follow up. But all this is completely out of our hands, so to worry about it is a waste of time.

SB: Did you have a clear sense of who your audience would be when you were making the film?

ET: Everyone.

ME: Somebody asked me at Chapter about the film represent-ing Wales and it attracting the kind of audience that would see that their country was capable of making particular kinds of films. In fact we haven't made this film to stand for anything, to represent anybody except ourselves. There are easier films to make for your first feature if you want to get your c.v. up or reach as big an audience as possible or whatever. I'm not trying to make it in to a heroic endeavour; it was hugely enjoyable. But if you make this kind of film you can't worry too much in advance about the audience in commercial terms. Somebody has to worry about it; but they have to sell the film that we have made and that's the kind of unspoken contract that you make. Despite all the trouble getting the film off the ground in advance we found that once we began making the film we were largely blissfully free of the kinds of pressures that people who make more expensive films come under.

SB: What kind of plans have you got now?

ET: We both had a kind of pact that it would be better for both of us to keep busy when the film was finished rather than hang around waiting to see what First Independent were going to do with it. Marc went straight into shooting *Resurrection Man* and I went into a six month period of writing a play and a film. We'd like to collaborate again, carry on the journey, it's hopefully not just a one off.

SB: You are both bilingual. How far is this a factor in what you do or plan to do?

ET: I feel at last that I am the same person in Welsh as I am in English. I used to feel more schizophrenic about it. I write more in English partly because my Welsh is not that good. Marc laughs at me. I would write in Welsh and English, there's no problem for me culturally. I just put words together better in English than in Welsh.

ME: I think if you're a writer you are likely to gravitate towards one language rather than the other. In terms of film-making it's a much easier position to be in. What I feel really bored with though is what I call the Kim Howells syndrome, and even Kevin Allen, though I know him and like him, saying that *Twin Town* will really upset the Tafia, and reading Kim Howells in *The New Statesman* saying Wales is run by the parlours of Pontcanna and the like. I think we've got to grow up a bit; having two languages shouldn't be a problem. Or at least if it's a problem it's a really interesting one to deal with. A European one if you like. The first film I made was in Welsh and in English with no subtitles and it was shown at The London Film Festival with no problem, though admittedly it was a short film without much dialogue in it. The idea of making it this way was that we do live with both languages and enshrined in both of them are different things that we feel about ourselves. We talk about some things in Welsh with some people and some things in English with others and if you translate that into film-making that can be extremely interesting. The Taviani brothers made a film which I always thought was a real lesson to us called *Padre Padrone* which was about the conflict between Sardinian and Italian when some Sardinian boys go to join the army in Italy. Now that's a really interesting internationally understandable film in which language is a function in the story. How you feel about home. How you feel about leaving. Like in *House* where you have the conflict between the American dream and just being Welsh. Hanging around being Welsh. I really feel we've got to stop marginalising each other. Not in any wide-eyed missionary way, it's just that it's boring now. Boring to complain about north and south, Welsh language and English language, valleys socialism versus rural nationalism; very boring to us and to the world outside. If you're going to talk about all this put it in the script as a tension which is interesting. We've liberated ourselves in a short time from a lot of things. When S4C started for example, we touched on it earlier in relation to *Pobol y Cwm*, how can you make an urban story entirely in Welsh and be taken seriously when you know that very few people in Cardiff speak Welsh. But you could make *Delicatessen* in Welsh. You could make a black and white science-fiction film in Welsh. It is not a problem. I just don't want any more late-night state of the nation chat shows discussing the problem of Welsh.

ET: This interview should really be about celebration. Anything but complaint. A lot of the people who write on these areas will be asking "What shall we do?" But Mark's right, a lot of those debates have already taken place, they are out of date, no longer part of the agenda. Mike Pearson from Brith Gof can no longer, for instance, go to Amsterdam and speak Welsh to an audience and call it a political act. Mike's a Welsh learner and a great artist who uses the muscle of speaking Welsh. Every time he's meant to speak he speaks the first ten sentences in Welsh and then stops and says that's my political statement then he answers the question. I find that now surplus to requirements. We no longer have to do that. I am a Welsh speaker who doesn't need that; we just need to dramatise the potential tensions. Like Marc said about *Padre Pardone*, that's a little bit of Sardinia made global. We can do that with Welsh.

ME: Two things related to this from our own experience: when Ed and I made *Silent Village* together we made the film 'back to back' for purely practical reasons because we needed the money from both the BBC and S4C. What's very interesting is that the two films are exactly the same except one version is in Welsh and the other is in English, but in another sense they are different films. They are different because of what the language makes you feel about that community. I think both versions are interesting. The second thing is, why we have to grow up a little bit in terms of how our culture is run, is to do with the good reasons for wanting an independent film culture in Wales. The BBC has its own agenda in Wales and there is no doubt as to where it thinks the 'true' Wales is, and that's in the Rhondda valley. And S4C has a political remit which is a clearer and more understandable problem in a way, their whole *raison d'etre* is to promote the Welsh language so which ever way they do it they have to make programmes which are in Welsh. So you have the situation where you cannot make a bilingual film in a country which is bilingual. So if there ever was an argument for an independent film sector it's here. Why can't I make a film in which there is as much Welsh or English in it as I need to tell the story? The BBC won't pay for it and S4C won't pay for it so where I am going to get the money in Wales? Here language almost defines the need for a film culture separate from television. I don't want to have to buy into their two versions of Wales when I make a film. I went to a Welsh language school and because there are certain values inscribed in the Welsh language we were encouraged to believe in a Wales that existed 'over there'; it was rural, it was green and everybody spoke Welsh and I was living in Cardiff and interested in Marvin Gaye records. I suddenly had a problem; if I liked Marvin Gaye and didn't recognise this green place where everyone spoke Welsh what did this say about my Welshness? It got to the point where I realised that it wasn't important any more. What is more interesting is making something that encompasses both of those experiences.

ET: It's a rich culture. There are two languages. If you speak Urdu and live on the south side of Cardiff you have three languages. All this is to be celebrated not to be defended. We have been in danger of defending and politicising ourselves out of creative existence.

ME: When you are a little bit younger you feel excluded from your culture because you don't know what it is and you don't know who you are. If you start blaming the establishment there are establishments in every culture. There is an argument for saying that in another country we might have had a crack at making a feature film a bit earlier. But you do what you can in the country that you care about and want to talk about. If I can do anything I would like to be helpful to anybody who now can't get an Arts Council grant for ten thousand quid. I really regret that that doesn't exist anymore. I'd love somebody to come to *House of America* and either say "I hate that, I don't want to make that. That's a thirty-five year old's film about Wales!" or say "Fucking hell they did it. How can I do it?" There are short film schemes coming through, but there has to be more money and organisation. It's not a cop out to say that's not my job, but I would certainly be very interested to talk to anybody who wants my opinion about it.

ET: It really is a different Wales now. Matthew Rees, young actor who comes out of RADA with lots of prizes, his first three jobs; he does *House of America* in his own accent. Then he does a second television film in the Welsh language. Third thing he walks in to the National Theatre and does a Peter Gill play about Cardiff in his own accent again. He will have no idea about the difference between that experience and what it was like for someone just ten years older. This change hasn't been created by the establishment or any strategy, though it might have happened faster if there had been one. It's happened through accidents and desire. Matthew and his generation are inheriting a fundamentally different Wales. And it's come about, as I said earlier, through a despite culture.

SB: I know it can sometimes sound a bit crass, but I wonder if we could finish by you talking about the kind of work that you have both admired and has become influential on you?

ME: What I was most interested in at school was painting. I went to University and did History of Art then sort of thought I'd go to art college. I discovered cinema almost as an obscure thing in the early 'eighties. I wasn't like an American or French person brought up on cinema. I knew television and pop music basically. Cinema was a European thing for me; watching these obscure European films that I had never heard of. I didn't arrive at film-making immersed in it. It was something I found out about quite late. As a result I started at the obscure end of it. The first thing that inspired me massively was the Bill Douglas Trilogy that they showed me at film college. For a while I just wanted to be Bill Douglas basically. When I made my first film the cameraman asked if I wanted any tracks and I said no I wanted everything static! Then somebody showed me a Pasolini film and I though that was amazing. These all sound like very arty influences because of where I had first come across film. I've come full circle now and I'm quite interested in the big commercial films from America.

ET: *The Discreet Charm of The Bourgeoisie*. The first blow-job I ever saw on the screen was in that film. The only things I had seen before that were *Superman* and *Star Wars* and everything else. This woman who lived in Brighton took me to these wacky joints where you saw all these other films. I thought it was all above me. Half of it did go straight by me but it was still fucking magic. You do things by default. I'm really a failed rugby player who started writing. Hopefully I'm a better writer than I would ever have been a rugby player.

ME: Even now a lot of the references that I naturally gravitate towards are from paintings and photographs. In *House* we nicked massively from Andrew Wyeth and Edward Hopper. To Americans this might be obvious, but hopefully here it's not.

ET: It's like daffodils and leeks to them. But it's the same argument for getting Pierre and George and for getting Steve to do Sid. It's like a bloke from Stoke for him. He says in one interview that the Welsh angle was what the Welsh want to make it for him; but he still wanted to do the film because he felt the fiction was good. And as a result he is believable as a Welsh character.

ME: If you are American any film is going to fit into a genre of which you have seen thousands of examples before, and we're jealous of them because they can access the Western, or subvert the Western or whatever. If you haven't got anything it's easier. Because it's a global culture you can do those things but in a way which is a bit more chaotic and not as steeped in the expertise of all that. But maybe more eclectic and interesting for that. **ET**: When I write scripts I start off with nothing to say. I've got absolutely zilch to say. I've got plenty to say in pubs and with friends, but nothing to say in scripts. My skill is to put words next to each other to make sentences which make ideas which hopefully make screenplays. They're possibilities. Through six or seven years of writing plays I've arrived at a photograph of nothing. I'm not interested in my point of view, I'm interested in the possibilities of fiction; if you put words together elegantly enough you create possibilities. What if? All life must be "what if" not "if you." That's why I believe in fiction. Not because I believe it's a panacea for all ills, but I believe in the life imagined. I hate myself when I have to shop in Kwik Save, there's no beauty to it. Waitrose is just Kwik Save with a bit of posh fucking dressing. Life imagined is where it's at. I'm always obsessed with dreamers. You have to arrive at nothing to say to arrive at everything to say. Directors and writers are paid to imagine not to reproduce.

SB: Ed and Marc thanks very much.

The Futures of Digital Television in Wales

Stuart Allan, Andrew Thompson
and Tom O'Malley

It is a case of trying to live in the future
and interpret it to the present.
Euryn Ogwen Williams[1]

Introduction

At first glance, there would appear to be very little by way of common ground being shared by the various media commentators proclaiming to know what the future is for digital terrestrial television (DTT) in Wales. Predictions about how DTT will be developed range from pessimistic assertions that it is a "dead-end technology," and thus one which will have a minimal effect on broadcasting as we know it, to excited pronouncements that it will usher in a technological revolution, fundamentally transforming the Welsh mediascape. At the same time, arguments that DTT will sound the death-knell for the current television networks are encountering other, equally confident, declarations that only DTT can ensure the long-term viability of institutions such as Sianel Pedwar Cymru (S4C).

A closer look at these competing projections of the future, however, reveals that there is a key assumption underpinning most of the corresponding scenarios: the current status quo of television broadcasting in Wales cannot hold for much longer. The primary aim of this chapter, therefore, is to critically assess the current state of development for DTT in general, and to consider the implications it may have for television broadcasting in Wales. In order to place DTT in an appropriate context, our investigation turns in the first instance to trace the historical development of broadcasting in Wales, with special attention being given to the role these institutions play in the promotion of Welsh identities. We proceed to examine the principal factors informing the implementation of DTT technology, which was launched in Wales in the autumn of 1998. Finally, several particularly salient issues for the future of Welsh television in the digital age are highlighted for further discussion and debate.

Broadcasting in Wales

From its inception in the 1920s, public broadcasting in Wales has been at the heart of a series of vigorous debates about the status – past and future – of the Welsh nation. Radio broadcasting was established under the aegis of the London-based British Broadcasting Company in 1922. In February 1923, the Cardiff station was brought into service and, on 1 March of that year, the first broadcast of a talk in the Welsh language took place. John Davies (1994: 50), in his book *Broadcasting and the BBC in Wales*, has gone so far as to assert that:

> It could be argued that the entire national debate in Wales, for fifty years and more after 1927 [the year the British Broadcasting Corporation was inaugurated], revolved around broadcasting, and that the other concessions to Welsh nationality won in those years were consequent upon the victories in the field of broadcasting.

The early years of broadcasting in Wales were marked by a number of different protests across Wales. Amongst the most vociferous of these voices were the interventions by the Welsh Academy, as well as those of Plaid Genedlaethol Cymru (the Welsh Nationalist Party).

At issue was the virtual absence of programmes regularly delivered through the medium of the Welsh language and, more broadly, with what was perceived to be broadcasting's complicity in promoting the 'anglicisation' of Wales. In this regard, Davies (1994: 48) cites W.J. Gruffydd, a prominent Welsh academic, who wrote in 1927 that "wireless is achieving the complete anglicisation of the intellectual life of the nation." In spite of such pronouncements, there was nevertheless a recognition on the part of many protesters that any solution to this problem must involve harnessing the powers of the new technology. Indeed, the voices of protest argued that Wales *must* have its own national wave-length. The absence of such a provision, in their view, called into question Wales's status as a nation; as one commentator wrote in the *Western Mail* in 1935: "Today, Wales, as a nation, is unique in Europe in that she has no wireless transmitter upon her soil. On a broadcast map of Europe Wales is blank" (cited in Lucas, 1981: 55). Concerns over the role of radio broad-casting in Wales were, to some extent, addressed in 1937, when the Welsh region began broadcasting for the first time on its own wavelength. The launch of the new Welsh Home Service in 1945, after regional broadcasting had been suspended during wartime, saw an increase in the number of programme hours produced in English and Welsh.

Following the end of the War, the debate over broadcasting in Wales, and in particular the question of Welsh language programming, moved to new terrain with the resumption of television broadcasts from Alexandra Palace in 1946. Prior to the launch of the Sutton Coldfield service in 1949, there had not been any television broadcasts in Wales, and for some – including many of those who had been active in the campaign for a Welsh radio broadcasting region – even this initial development was too much. As with radio before, the advent of television in Wales was met by concerns that the arrival of English language 'mass culture' would herald the end of Welsh language culture. Indeed, even when the Wenvoe television station opened in South Wales in 1952, Lady Megan Lloyd-George, who had been a prominent figure in the campaign for independent Welsh broadcasting, signalled that this was only the beginning; she made it clear that, in her view, within the UK each 'separate nation' should have a television station of its own (cited in Davies, 1994: 175). The launch of the independent Television Wales and West (TWW) Company in 1958 injected further life into the debate on broadcasting in Wales, in general, and Welsh language broadcasting, in particular. By the late 1950s, the general competition for viewers was forcing the BBC to adapt to the new television environment; in Wales, part of this competition, albeit not the main concern, was centred on the Welsh language viewer.

If the genesis of the television age in Wales had initially engendered considerable anxiety amongst some Welsh commentators, by the early 1960s it was the demand for a greater utilisation of the Welsh language on Welsh television (and radio) which spurred on a new generation of language activists. Indeed, it was a BBC Welsh Annual Radio Lecture by Saunders Lewis, a former president of Plaid Genedlaethol Cymru, and one of those who, in the early 1950s, had warned of the potentially destructive impact of television on Welsh culture (Davies, 1994), which provided the spark for the formation of Cymdeithas Yr Iaith Gymraeg (the Welsh Language Society, hereafter CYIG) in 1962. Lewis, in his lecture entitled 'Tynged Yr Iaith' (The Fate of the Language), had remarked that "the language is more important than self-government", and went on to explain that a campaign to "restore" the Welsh language was "only possible through revolutionary methods" (cited in Butt-Philip, 1975: 90). Although Lewis had not focused specifically on the issue of broadcasting in Wales in the course of his lecture, the "revolutionary methods" which he had advocated – which consisted of unlawful non-violent direct action – were adopted by CYIG when engaging with the broadcasting authorities (the first campaign staged by the CYIG was a sit-in at BBC Wales's studio in Bangor on 29 November, 1968).

In the late 1960s and early 1970s, CYIG also drafted a number of documents proposing the establishment of a Welsh fourth channel. Central to the proposals made by CYIG was that broadcasting in Wales should promote the cultural distinctiveness of the Welsh nation. In *Broadcasting in Wales – To enrich or destroy our national life?*, CYIG argued:

> It would appear that the function of radio and TV programmes is two-fold; firstly they should reflect the spirit, civilization and enable the people to develop their own particular genius [...] In reality, English is the language of broadcasting in Wales and TV and radio sets are being used to Anglicise our homes and kill our language. A Welsh man [sic] is thus educated to look at life through English eyes (cited in Tomos, 1982: 40).

The potential for a Welsh fourth channel had been raised earlier in the decade, albeit through an intimation toward a second ITV channel, as a result of the publication of the report of the Pilkington Committee in 1962. Whilst the latter idea was rejected by the incoming Labour government, it was nevertheless pursued by various groups in the form of bids for an ITV-2 and a Fourth Channel (Blanchard, 1982: 8-10).

Subsequent to the establishment of BBC Wales in 1964, and the emergence of Harlech Television in 1968 as the sole independent television company in Wales (replacing Television Wales and West), the issue of programming through the medium of Welsh received a renewed impetus. Still, clashes over the allocation of hours for Welsh language programmes (and their time-tabling), as well as complaints from non Welsh-speakers about the spread of Welsh language programmes over both networks, generated considerable public dissatisfaction with the present arrangement (Thomas, 1971; Davies, 1994). In addition, from the position of CYIG, which by the late 1960s and early 1970s was devoting much of its collective energies towards the campaign for a Welsh fourth channel, neither network had satisfactorily utilised the Welsh language in their programmes. And yet, in spite of this charge, BBC Wales itself was accused of providing too much coverage of the activities of CYIG, and thus promoting the society's campaign. Moreover, according to one Welsh Labour MP, it was also guilty of demonstrating a bias towards Plaid Cymru (Davies, 1994: 287).

It was the publication of two reports during the 1970s, however, which substantively advanced the idea of a Welsh fourth channel. The first resulted from the Crawford Committee inquiry set up by the Heath government in 1973. It recommended in its 1974 report that a fourth channel in Wales would provide the solution to the question of how best to address the issue of Welsh language programming. The second report, that of the Annan Committee in 1977, reiterated the conclusions of the previous report. Throughout this period, and in particular in the discussions over the findings of the two committees, a central feature of the debate on broadcasting in Wales had been the desire, on the part of those involved, to prevent any future hostility between Welsh-speakers and non-Welsh-speakers over the issue of Welsh-language broadcasting. Nevertheless, it was also evident, particularly in the aftermath of the devolution referendum in 1979, that for some commentators the use of the Welsh language in broadcasting was associated with a nationalist politic. The *Western Mail*, for example, contended that the rejection of a Welsh Assembly also represented a rejection of the demand for a Welsh fourth channel (Davies, 1994: 340; see also Briggs, 1995).

The establishment of Sianel Pedwar Cymru (S4C) in 1980 took place after Gwynfor Evans, a former president of Plaid Cymru, had threatened to go on a hunger strike until the government reversed its decision not to go ahead with the promised channel. Credit for its formal inauguration in 1982 was similarly due to a persistent, high-profile campaign conducted by CYIG and, to a lesser extent, Plaid Cymru. That the campaign to establish S4C has been closely linked to the politics of the Welsh language and, by association, with the nationalist movement, has ensured that the channel and its governing body, the Welsh Fourth Channel Authority, have been subject to claims of political bias towards Plaid Cymru (Davies, 1994). Moreover, criticism has been directed towards S4C's representation of Wales and the Welsh; as Michelle Ryan (1986: 186) writes:

> whilst some of their output [...] is beginning to display some awareness of the importance of addressing contemporary issues that relate specifically to Wales [...] the bulk of their programmes appear dated, conservative and stereotyped. Too much of their drama and features refer back in an uncritical way to a Welsh mythical past or else provides soap opera with a Welsh voice.

Another, more recent commentator (Griffiths, 1993), whilst acknowledging some of the above problems with S4C's representation of Welshness, has nevertheless noted the pioneering role of other Welsh language programmes in exploring the complexity of Welsh identity (see also Bevan, 1984).

S4C, as the only outlet for Welsh language television, represents a crucially important cultural institution in Wales. In 1997, for example, an average of 30 hours per week of Welsh language programming was shown on the channel. Moreover, through new music and lifestyle programmes directed towards younger Welsh-speakers, as well through soap operas and films,

S4C occupies a pivotal position in creating the space for a continual re-negotiation of diverse forms of Welsh identity. At the same time, as a co-producer of films, as well as through the commissioning of programmes from independent producers, S4C has also enjoyed notable successes in exporting the Welsh language to an audience outside of Wales. Now that S4C has secured the contract to operate a digital delivery system – in conjunction with Channel 5 – the ability to continue to expand its audience beyond the borders of Wales will be a vital element for the future development of the company. As Euryn Ogwen Williams, digital development consultant for S4C, explains: "we are a Welsh company that will be operating on a UK and European level" (cited in Hughes, 1998: 23). In this venture, promoting the Welsh dimension of the company will be a central plank of its operations.

There are, however, a number of problems with respect to this new role for S4C. In the first instance, the fact that S4C is primarily a commissioning broadcaster, and not a fully-fledged programme producer, limits its degree of autonomy in the realm of programme content. BBC Wales supplies S4C with ten hours of its Welsh programming, whilst the rest is commissioned from HTV and other independent producers. Similarly, in terms of its news and current affairs, the former are produced by BBC Wales and the latter by HTV. Additionally, there is the issue of S4C's relationship with the forces which brought it into existence. Angharad Tomos (1982: 52), in describing the founding of the channel in 1980, writes that "the Welsh had transformed the campaign from simply one for a TV Channel to one of national revival." Others have offered similar perspectives, arguing that S4C has played an important function in easing divisions between Welsh-speakers and non-Welsh-speakers living in Wales and thus facilitating the promotion of the Welsh language. As Geraint Stanley Jones, a former controller of BBC Wales and chief executive of S4C from 1989-1994, argues: "S4C has had many successes, but the huge success is the social one. It's allowed social harmony to flourish where it didn't before. Why is it in the past ten years so many people have been learning Welsh?" (cited in Horton, 1996: 16).

Wales Past: in the Oscar-nominated *Hedd Wyn* and *Elenya*.

Wales Present: Ceri Sherlock explores Welshness through the myth of *Branwen* and the shockingly contemporary in *Dafydd*.

Mapping Wales: Endaf Emlyn's odyssey through sexuality, politics and madness in *Gadael Lenin* and *Un Nos Ola Leuad*.

Young Wales: alienation in the much acclaimed *House of America* and *Streetlife*, Karl Francis's film of urban relations.

Political Wales: two differing approaches to an increasingly popular subject. BBC Wales and Trevor Griffiths took the biopic route in *Food for Ravens*; HTV offered the National Assembly thriller *In the Company of Strangers*.

Made in Wales: striking a balance between imported and indigenous talent remains central to production and distribution. *Trip Trap* brought in Kevin Whateley, while native Philip Madoc proved a popular detective.

Yoof Wales: do *Pam Fi Duw* and *Human Traffic* represent two sides of the same Welsh coin?

Cartoon Wales: in fact an international industry, as *Billy the Cat* and *The Canterbury Tales* suggest.

For S4C, the future depends on its ability to retain the support of Welsh-speakers and non-Welsh-speakers alike, a task which might prove to be much more difficult to perform than has been the case in the past. Our discussion now turns to consider the implications of 'the digital television revolution' for television in Wales.

The Advent of Digital Television

What is digital television? A response to this question restricted to the level of the technology itself is relatively straightforward. Briefly, DTT dispenses with analogue frequencies, which are capable of carrying only one signal – and therefore only one television channel. The advent of digital technology dramatically increases the number of channels each terrestrial (land-based) frequency can carry and, moreover, enhances the accuracy of their transmission. It converts sounds and pictures into an electronic code of binary digits which has the effect of compressing the signal so that each frequency can carry far greater amounts of information. This combination of different television channels on the same frequency, a feat achieved through computer technology, is called 'multiplexing'. It follows that eventually, in perhaps ten to fifteen years, analogue transmissions of terrestrial broadcast services may be 'switched off' so as to free up the electromagnetic spectrum for other types of users, such as cellular telephone companies.

Precisely what this means for the television viewer, however, continues to be a matter of considerable dispute. In general, most commentators anticipate that DTT will provide, firstly, a plethora of new channels, both nationally and locally, 'at the flick of a switch'. Estimates vary, but some advocates are optimistic that over 30 channels will be available when the service is launched, with many more to follow. Secondly, digital technology should provide a much improved television picture, particularly for portable television units, and 'CD-quality' sound. Thirdly, it is expected that a host of new services, ranging from 'widescreen' television (screen dimensions proportional to 16 by 9) to 'super-teletext' facilities, will emerge. And finally, through the use of a telephone return link, DTT has the potential to make possible 'interactive' news, education, information and entertainment services. Viewers would be able to, for example, access the 'information superhighway' via Internet pages on their television, engage in home shopping and banking, call up entertainment programming and films on demand (usually for a fee registered by using a 'smartcard'), consult an electronic programme guide, and so forth.

In order to receive digital terrestrial television, viewers will have two options. New digital television sets, which are also compatible with analogue services, are due to become available in retail outlets very shortly. To be initially priced at around £1,000 a piece, this is the more expensive of the two options (newspaper reports suggest that Panasonic is producing digital television sets in Cardiff). For those individuals unwilling or unable to replace their current television, there is the option of purchasing a separate 'set-top decoder box' for about £200, a price heavily subsidised by the main digital players. These boxes are designed to allow existing television sets to handle digital frequencies. Regardless of which option is chosen, viewers will have 'open access' to those programmes being 'simulcast' on analogue frequencies, that is, the 'free to air' services (funded by the licence fee or advertising). However, certain other services, possibly including 'special events' programming ('live' sports are especially significant here) or specialised business or financial information, will be financed by subscription or a 'pay per view' policy. In this way, 'conditional access' is restricted to those customers who are willing to pay for these exclusive types of programming.

In attempting to establish a legislative framework to oversee the development of DTT, the Conservative Government released a White Paper, entitled *Digital Terrestrial Television: The Government's Proposals* (DTB, 1995), in August, 1995. This document commences by outlining the Government's principal policy concerns regarding the allocation of the spectrum to different users, and for the licensing and regulation of transmission and broadcasting. At stake, it declares, is the need to:

ensure that viewers and listeners are able to choose from a wide variety of terrestrial television channels and national and local radio stations; give existing national broadcasters the opportunity to develop digital services and so safeguard public service broadcasting into the digital age; give terrestrial broadcasters the opportunity to compete with those on satellite and cable; help a fair and effective market to develop; help UK manufacturers and producers compete at home and overseas; and make best use of the available spectrum (DTB, 1995: 1).

There is a clear sense in this White Paper that the Government is attempting to act quickly. An emphasis is placed throughout the document on the rapid speed at which DTT is developing, and the significance of ensuring that British companies are effectively positioned to exploit the new technologies as they are introduced. Insisting that there is a "strong consensus in the industry" that DTT is "commercially viable", the document proceeds to make explicit the Government's commitment to encouraging competitive market forces to "unlock an important and exciting industrial opportunity" (DTB, 1995: 4; see also Brookes, 1996).

Although digital broadcasting via satellite or cable has been allowed since 1990, it was the 1996 Broadcasting Act which extended the necessary provision to licence digital terrestrial television frequencies. Specifically, the Act empowers the Independent Television Commission (ITC) to oversee the emergence of the new terrestrial digital services (the Radio Authority performs this function for digital terrestrial radio), although Oftel, the telecoms regulator, currently looks after conditional access and interactive services. In essence, the ITC is charged with the responsibility for licensing and regulating the respective multiplex operators, the programme makers, and the providers of additional digital services, including teletext and computer data services. Accordingly, it possesses the power to monitor performance within criteria set down by the Government. These criteria have been invoked, in turn, to establish that groups of digital channels would be brought together into six separate blocks, or 'multiplexes'. Each of these multiplexes can carry at least three television channels, plus additional data services. This strategy ensures, at least in principle, that the different broadcasters will have to compete in order to have their channel (or channels) supplied through a multiplex provider. It is this competition over access to the multiplexes which, according to advocates of this policy, guarantees that the actual programming being broadcast will be of a high quality. More sceptical voices maintain, in contrast, that a greater number of channels does not necessarily translate into wider viewer choice.

The 1996 Act allocated Multiplex 1 to the BBC and Multiplex 2 to a joint bid from Channel 3 (ITV) and Channel 4. Sharing Multiplex 3 are S4C, Channel 5 and several broadcasters supplying Gaelic programmes in Scotland. In each case, the multiplexes will carry digital versions of the established terrestrial channels, plus new digital services (DTT, 1996). The other three multiplexes were advertised and awarded in the summer of 1997. All three of the licences were awarded to a consortium, British Digital Broadcasting (BDB), led by the two major forces in UK commercial television, Carlton Communications and Granada Group. Digital Television Network (DTN), the other contender for the DDT licences, has recently lodged a formal complaint with the European Commission, evidently over the bidding process. The principal backers of DTN are the US-owned cable operator NTL (through a consortium) and United News and Media. The satellite television company British Sky Broadcasting (BSkyB), in which Rupert Murdoch's News Corporation holds a 40 per cent stake, had been forced by the ITC to pull out of the consortium due to alarm over the concentration of ownership in the industry. More recently, BDB has announced plans to provide 12 subscription channels at a basic rate and three at a premium rate, from mid-1998. Significantly, BSkyB has now secured a long-term arrangement with BDB to supply it with programming content (most of which, in the form of film, sports and US material, it will purchase from others), thereby raising new allegations of unfair competition. That is to say, BSkyB's programming commitments, together with its involvement in encryption and subscriber management, amounts to a daunting degree of control in the eyes of many critics.

The news that S4C had won the contract to operate the Multiplex 3 digital terrestrial television service sparked a delighted response from some quarters in the industry, with some even suggesting that it had secured a 'licence to print money' (Hughes, 1998: 23). S4C's successful bid, advanced under a new company name of S4C Digital Networks (SDN) Ltd, constitutes a co-operative venture with United News and Media, owner of HTV, and NTL, which is controlled by CableTel (the third largest cable operator in the UK). Plans being developed by S4C through its SDN subsidiary reportedly include a bilingual 'Digital College' providing programmes for those learning the Welsh language. In addition, SDN promised in its application for a multiplex service licence to deliver to its audience an English language pre-school nursery channel, the content for which will be made in Wales; the Turner Entertainment channel, which draws on Time Warner programming from the US; a motoring channel, to be produced by ITN; an information channel, carrying news, sport, entertainment, weather and travel content, once again in conjunction with ITN; a nature channel, which offers live monitoring of different animals in their natural habitat through remote-controlled cameras (evidently to be supplied by Welsh independent Teliesyn) and, finally, a channel for Gaelic language programmes (SDN, 1997). All of these additional services, some of which will be 'free-to-air' whilst others paid for through subscription, are to be provided as UK-wide services.

"We are pushing the idea that we are a totally Welsh company that reaches out into the world," declares S4C's digital development consultant (cited in Hughes, 1998: 23). The primary purpose behind the digital initiative, not surprisingly, is to make sufficient profits to ensure the future development of its services. In his words:

> The big problem about judging just how much it will make depends to a large extent on the take-up of digital television. It may not make megabucks but it will make money, certainly by the year 2010 [the likely date when the present analogue channels will come to an end]. And it will fund more and more of the pay services and help develop new ideas as we go along (cited in Hughes, 1998: 23).

This highly optimistic scenario notwithstanding, some critics are insisting that the digitalisation of broadcasting threatens the very future of a distinctive mediascape in Wales, particularly where its creative production communities are concerned.

Our attention turns in the next section to consider several particularly important policy issues which have the potential to profoundly shape the future of television in Wales in the wake of the digital revolution.

Key Issues for Digital Television in Wales

For the foreseeable future, digital television – whether on terrestrial, cable or satellite platforms – will be available exclusively to those who are sufficiently well-off in financial terms to afford it. Critics of the new technology point to the imminent emergence of a new 'television underclass' made up of people left behind by the digital revolution, that is, people unable to purchase the essential set-top boxes, let alone a new digital television set. Indeed, the current licence fee is beyond the means of many people living in Wales on low incomes, with large fines and, in some cases, prison sentences waiting for those who fail to pay. This situation has the potential to worsen as 'universal access' is increasingly being redefined by economic factors. If the benefits of the 'information age' are to be made available for all, the Government will have to act to override market forces.

Chris Smith, the Labour Minister for Culture, Media and Sport, stated in a speech to the Royal Television Society that: "Broadcasting, as its very name implies, offers benefits to the many rather than the few. I want to ensure universal access to the current free-to-air public service channels, and I want that access to be through digital services" (cited in Brown, 1997: 4). This statement, whilst encouraging, leaves unanswered the question as to why viewers should have to invest in a set-top box or digital television in order to watch, for example, the BBC programming which they have already paid for through their licence fee. Similarly, we need to ask what happens to a collective sense of shared national identity when the television audience splinters into an array of fragments in the multi-channel universe? These types of questions throw into sharp relief the corporatist assumptions underpinning a national broadcasting policy which is becoming increasingly driven by commercial considerations, rather than public service ones. Indeed, Smith's own comments reveal that he is at least aware of the potential dangers of digital television in this regard, if not sufficiently moved to intervene as of yet: "I certainly regard television as a key element – if not *the* key element in our national culture.... It is television that for many provides the main source of cultural excitement and the main window on what the nation and the world has to offer" (cited in Brown, 1997: 4).

This reference to the importance of television for a national culture strikes a significant resonance for those engaged in debates about the future of public service broadcasting in Wales. For those who are deeply concerned about these issues, media baron Rupert Murdoch symbolises many of their worst fears. Murdoch has made no secret of his intentions to lead the digital transformation of television in the UK, thereby earning the name 'digital dictator' by some critics. His direction of the satellite company BSkyB has allowed him to assume a controlling position in the digital marketplace and, moreover, currently provides him with the potential means to drive many of his competitors out of business. In many ways these developments parallel ongoing efforts to dominate other media sectors. Critics have long alleged, for example, that funds derived from BSkyB are being spent on Murdoch's newspaper operations so as to severely undercut the profitability of rival titles. This tactic of cross-subsidy has seen sales of *The Times* undergo a substantive rise, primarily at the expense of *The Independent* and *The Daily Telegraph*, at the same time that it is arguably becoming the biggest loss-maker of all time in British newspaper history (see Toynbee, 1998: 17). The range of Murdoch titles claims about 40 per cent of the country's newspaper readership, and yet few doubt that this strategy of predatory pricing will eventually lead to a further concentration of control. Not surprisingly, News International strenuously denies these allegations, but they are nevertheless forming a basis for a new Competition Bill currently making its way through Parliament (unlike the situation in Europe and the US, this type of predatory pricing is not illegal in Britain). Chances that the Bill will eventually be implemented appear to be slim, however, in no small part due to the influence Murdoch enjoys at 10 Downing Street.[3]

Easily the most profitable broadcaster in the UK, BSkyB registered more than £300 million in pre-tax profits in the financial year ending 30 June, 1997, and had revenues exceeding £31.2 billion (Horsman, 1997: 4). And yet, only a tiny fraction of the revenues being generated is finding its way into new programming – the programme making budget for Sky 1, its flagship channel, was about £36 million in 1996 – as pressures mount to boost shareholder dividends. The number of British subscribers to its satellite and cable services is currently over 6 million, with Sky 1 available in approximately 25 per cent of households. In seeking to further commandeer market share, BSkyB is currently promising to launch a 200-channel digital satellite service by the end of 1998. Eventually, as the analogue terrestrial system gives way to a digital one, the company will be effectively positioned to offer its services to the majority of households: projections are for 50 per cent of homes by 2002, and 75 per cent by 2010 (McCann, 1998: 3). Underlying this expansion is a crucial shift away from subscriptions to advertising, thereby posing an even greater challenge to the revenues of the ITV companies (expected to be particularly hard-hit are their programme-making budgets). In the meantime, however, critics are disturbed by the potential for BSkyB to cross-subsidise its digital pay-TV activities in ways which undercut the ability of rival companies to compete. Moreover, they are also fearful that BSkyB's advantage will be further extended through its ability to constrain the access of these very same competitors by virtue of its involvement in the ongoing development of the digital subscription technologies.

BSkyB is, of course, only one of several large communications groups actively positioning themselves to dominate the converging spheres of broadcasting, telecommunications and information technology. Others include British Telecom (BT), British Digital Broadcasting (Carlton and Granada's digital television joint-venture), and Microsoft. Significantly, however, each of these companies, at different levels, is either involved – or attempting to get involved – with one or more of the others. The links between BSkyB and BDB, as noted above, revolve around the former's commitment to providing the latter with programming, especially top sporting events such as live boxing matches and Premier League football. At the same time, an enhanced relationship between BSkyB and BT has recently come under attack from the European Commission, which is warning that it might block their joint venture into interactive home shopping and banking services. Meanwhile, the US company Microsoft, via its subsidiary WebTV, is poised to break into the UK broadcasting market through its development of a new digital service which will allow viewers to effectively turn their television sets into personal computers. Microsoft is determined to have its software packaged as part of the set-top decoder box being launched by BDB, thereby further blurring the lines between these separate companies.

For the BBC, one 'efficiency drive' after another has been launched in order to cut funds from conventional Corporate budgets to pay for the Multiplex 1 services (revenues derived from the recent privatisation of its transmitter network were invested in digital technology). As the digital revolution unfolds, the BBC is moving quickly to establish commercial partners in order to extend its digital services. UKTV, for example, has been set up as a joint venture with Flextech, a pay television 'packager' which is part of Tele-Communications Inc International (TCII), the US cable company. The plan is to provide an array of channels featuring BBC programming (an existing example of which is UK Gold, composed primarily of material drawn from the Corporation's back-catalogue, which has been available on satellite and cable since 1992). Also under negotiation is a joint arrangement with Discovery, another channel provider controlled by TCII. It is intended that a series of BBC-Discovery channels will be aimed at television markets around the globe (Horsman, 1998: 2-3). Some BBC managers are maintaining that the increasing commercialisation of the Corporation in both its structure and activities is essential if public service broadcasting is to survive in the new era. It is arguably the case, however, that as external competition from programme makers intensifies, the financial reasons for the BBC maintaining a production arm will diminish. Fears have been expressed that the day when a fully privatised BBC has been transformed into a pay service, offering news, documentary and non-entertainment programming, is not far off. John Birt, Director-General of the BBC and a keen advocate of digital television, was cautiously guarded about the future. In his words:

"The who, the how and the when of the digital age remain crucial questions for Britain. Our prosperity, jobs – even our cultural identity – depend on getting the answers right" (cited in Peak and Fisher, 1996: 180).

In the case of the ITV network, those answers appear to be just as elusive. The competition unleashed after the most recent franchise round has increased pressure on companies to achieve economies of scale through take-overs. In Wales, this led to the acquisition of the HTV Group by United News and Media for a reported £3372 million agreed bid in 1997 (Able, 1998: 24; Smith, 1997a, 1997b). A phase of corporate 'restructuring' immediately followed the purchase, the result of which meant job 'redundancies' in Cardiff and Bristol. Managing Director Malcolm Wall, whilst pointing out that pressures would only increase in the years to come because of an evermore competitive environment, does see the "high production standards of the Welsh service" to be worthy of further support: "We believe Wales is in a unique position with a talent base which has not been fully developed" (cited in Able, 1998: 24). Precisely what form this development will take remains to be seen, but what is certain is that new programming is contingent on advertising revenues which are being evermore thinly split as channels proliferate. Peter Elias Jones, ex-director of programmes at HTV, regards the advent of digital television as a crucial vehicle for change in that it will allow independent Welsh companies to provide a "panoply of programme styles." Still, in his view: "Nobody yet knows how to expand, however, as the other side of the millennium is digital and the abyss." He then proceeds to make a comment which places an otherwise optimistic forecast about new jobs in the industry in a decidedly bleak light: "Digital means volume and cheapness; it's chewing-gum television ... and that means greater and greater opportunities" (cited in Gow, 1997: 16).

S4C has over the years proven to be popular with Welsh language speakers and has most certainly enhanced the status of the language itself. This tradition of public service is going to be severely challenged, however, by the emergence of a digitalised delivery system and what is an increasingly market-oriented broadcasting policy environment. Reportedly by the end of 1998, for example, just as S4C is made available throughout the UK, Channel 4 will be broadcast throughout Wales for the first time via digital television. Some commentators have argued that this will mean, in turn, that S4C will have to respond with much more English language programming if it is to retain its audience share. Whether or not S4C does indeed go down this path, it is likely to experience a decline in its viewership figures which may only get worse as it faces more and more competition from other digital operators. Once all of its services are transferred to digital and, like other terrestrial providers, it loses its current analogue frequency, some fear that it may simply become a provider of Welsh language programmes to a very small domestic niche market and, through satellite, to an even smaller international audience. Despite the upbeat rhetoric being generated by S4C's spokespeople about its digital future, it is far from clear whether it will be able to continue to fulfil its remit in a multi-channel world.

Significantly, despite the new digital service it is planning, S4C will have no more state funding in real terms than in 1997. Moreover, and in accordance with its 12-year license agreement, it must provide digital Welsh language services free to Wales and, in future, any English language material has to be funded from sources 'other than our public funds.' As competition between S4C and other commercial television companies intensifies, it will take a strong campaign to retain current levels of state funding – around £69 million in 1995. Cries of "level playing field" and "unfair competition" will be heard if S4C is successful in using its subsidy base from the Treasury to establish services that draw audiences from its rivals. Even the current situation provides an indication of the type of difficulties which are looming over the horizon. For example, viewers living in Cardiff relying on 'off air' broadcasting have access to five channels, one of which is S4C (unless, of course, an extra aerial has been installed and pointed at Bristol to receive Channel 4). For those viewers who do not speak Welsh, which is the majority in Cardiff, they will nevertheless encounter the Welsh language on a regular basis as they switch between channels in search of something to watch. The status of S4C, we would argue, plays a profound role in creating a sense of place, an awareness of living in Wales as a distinct nation. For most, Cardiff viewers subscribing to CableTel's service, however, they will only encounter S4C if they choose channel number 98 on their remote control. S4C is obviously still there to be watched for those purposely seeking it out, but its presence – and with it a larger perception of national identity – is dramatically diminished.

For over two generations Welsh language activists have focused on gaining influence over broadcasting on the grounds that access to these institutions would deliver a national audience to a nationalist agenda. As the attendant technology changes, so the assumption that television can continue to perform this crucial task of promoting Welsh identities becomes increasingly problematic. Public service broadcasting, with its commitment to sustaining a forum for a richly diverse array of contending ideas, beliefs and viewpoints to circulate from across Wales, is incompatible with the ethos of 'the market' so readily endorsed by the digital companies. If, as one advocate quoted above suggests, digital means "chewing-gum television," then the drive to maximise revenue in this sector must not be allowed to silence the distinctive cultural voices which make up the substance of Welsh identities. Recent policy statements made by S4C have not shied away from expressing a strong desire to be a UK-wide player; its own projection of its future in the digital era, it readily concedes, is being primarily defined within commercial parameters. It is these very same parameters, we would argue, that will have to be drastically recast if S4C's role in promoting Welsh culture is going to be preserved.

Conclusion

If, indeed, we are currently witnessing the dawn of the digital age in Wales, then the time to involve ourselves in these changes is now. In this brief account of several key factors informing the development of digital terrestrial television in Wales, we have sought to highlight a basis for further debate. For a variety of reasons, not least of which is the intrinsically complex nature of the dynamics involved and the speed at which they are unfolding, there has been very little by way of public discussion of these issues in Wales to date. Rather alarmingly, much of the news coverage of DTT, such as that found in publications like the *Western Mail,* has been largely restricted to the business pages. There attention tends to focus on the financial aspects of the main DTT players as they scramble to capitalise on new developments. Only rarely is it the case that news stories concerning DTT are finding their way onto the main news agenda, a problem which must be addressed if we are hear those alternative voices from outside the business community who are struggling to be heard. Everyone living in Wales has a stake in how the 'digital television revolution' is managed, and yet the opportunities for ordinary people to contribute to public debate are severely restricted.

The future of public service broadcasting in Wales, as we have attempted to demonstrate here, is at risk. Now is the time to intervene to both protect and enrich this tradition of 'public service' for tomorrow.

Notes

1. Digital development consultant for S4C.
2. Elsewhere, we have examined the cultural dynamics of Welsh national identities in relation to the newspaper press in the latter decades of the nineteenth century.

References

L. Able, "Departed winds of change improve picture at HTV," *Wales 2000 Western Mail,* February 1998, p.24.

D. Bevan, 'The Mobilization of Cultural Minorities: The Case of Sianel Pedwar Cymru," *Media, Culture and Society,* 6, pp.103-117.

A. Bevins, "Twin threat to Blair as ministers are told to oppose controls on newspaper price war," The Independent, 9 February, p.4.

S. Blanchard, "Where Do New Channels Come From?" in S. Blanchard, and D. Mornely (eds), *What's this Channel Fo(u)r? An Alternative Report,* (Comedia: London, 1982).

A. Briggs, *The History of Broadcasting in the United Kingdom Volume v. Competition,* (Oxford University Press: Oxford, 1995).

R. Brookes, "Report on Digital Terrestrial Broadcasting White Paper," *Communcations Law,* Vol. I, No. 1, 1996, pp.38-40.

R. Brown, "Media Column," *The Independent,* 29 September, 1997, p.4.

A. Butt-Philip, *The Welsh Question: Nationalism in Welsh Politics 1945-1970,* (University of Wales Press: Cardiff:, 1975).

J. Davies, (University of Wales Press: Cardiff:, 1994).

Department of National Heritage, (MHMSO: London:, 1996). *Digital Terrestrial Broadcasting: The Government's Proposals.*

Between Nation and Animation: the Fear of a Mickey Mouse Planet

Tim Robins & Chris Webster

Animation has reached more screens in more countries than any other product of Wales' media industries. From the beginning, the figures have been impressive. *SuperTed* was dubbed into 17 languages and sold to 45 countries, while more recently *Shakespeare – The Animated Tales* has been screened in 50 countries and 60% of the UK's secondary schools. Recognition has also come in the form of industry awards and the interest of the world's largest media companies. *Animation Classics' Hamlet* and *A Winter's Tale* have won US Primetime Emmy Awards for Best Animation; *Gogs*, Aaargh Animation's anarchic Stone Age family, has won 20 awards including best animation at the 1997 Chicago and New York film and television festivals. Yet, despite their success, it has been hard to identify such products as distinctively Welsh.

Some critics have suggested that the animation industry's involvement with international production, distribution and consumption has resulted in an homogenized, global product that lacks a Welsh identity. For others, animation's sometimes garish form, profane content and popularist appeal are enough to preclude it as a suitable vehicle for the celebration of the cultural life of Wales.

Our aim in this chapter is to explore and take issue with these views. We argue that the relationships between the animation industry, Wales and the world and between animation, Wales and Welshness are more complex than the simple oppositions between the local and the global, between high and low culture, allow. Instead, we trace some of the complex social, cultural, economic and political relationships that shape the production of animation in Wales.

Although we focus on the economic structures that support the country's industry, we recognise that animation is more than a commodity to be exchanged in the market place. Animation, like novels, poetry, drama, film, television and radio can provide a resource for the narration of nationhood and the imagining of cultural identities. But here again, we seek to address, if not answer, the complex issues around how a national culture can be represented on screen and how such representations are to be evaluated.

Our account is unavoidably partial. There are a number of reasons for this. Animation encompasses a wide range of media products and practices. As a term, it can refer to a range of techniques used to bring movement or 'life' to otherwise inanimate materials such as pencil drawings, clay and computer images. These techniques can, in turn, be used for a wide range of representational forms from slapstick comedy to more abstract, aesthetic works. Added to this, there have been few attempts to document the structure of the industry in Wales: how many production companies exist, their geographical distribution and how many people they employ.

Our starting point is the advent of S4C, partly because the development of an animation industry in Wales has been integral to the broadcaster's aims. From the beginning of Wales's fourth channel, animation had a number of obvious appeals. It was a popular technique for entertainment and, unlike Channel Four, S4C's programming was intended to be explicitly popularist. Animation was relatively easy to dub into English or any other language for that matter, so as a product, it had an immediate, reasonably accessible market beyond S4C's Welsh speaking audience. S4C was also intended to foster the development of the independent media sector in Wales and animation production was part of that sector.

The animation industry also provided S4C with one of its first major successes, *SuperTed*, the adventures of a magical bear and his alien companion Spotty. The production brought together talent from Wales and England and was designed and directed by Dave Edwards who had worked on commercials and feature films such as *The Yellow Submarine*. *SuperTed* had a budget to match this commercial background. Costing an estimated £80,000 an episode (in 1983), *SuperTed* was a glossy, relatively expensive, commercially attractive series that could be recognised by the industry and viewers as a quality product. The programme became an international success. It was dubbed into 17 languages and sold to 45 countries. The rights to screen *SuperTed's* three seasons of stories were bought by The Disney Channel and the right to produce new *SuperTed* adventures was bought by Hanna-Barbera.

"*SuperTed* did what it needed to do for us," says S4C's current commissioning editor for animation, Chris Grace. "It established S4C as an animation commissioner at a very high level." S4C's commission also helped establish Siriol as a small production company organized along the lines of a traditional animation studio with a permanent staff and facilities, such as a paint and trace shop. Siriol also originated other, albeit less high profile (though nonetheless popular) series such as *Wil Cwac Cwac.*

Siriol Animation was to remain the main beneficiary of S4C funding throughout the 'eighties, although S4C also supported other studios and productions, notably *Hanner Dusin,* created by Tony Barnes, and work by independent animators such as Joanna Quinn (*Girls Night Out)* and Clive Walley (*Quartet).* However, *SuperTed* in particular confronted Siriol and S4C with the possibilities and difficulties of local animation production. Further attempts to develop the *SuperTed* franchise foundered with a coolly received stage musical and a never-to-be-made feature film. Eventually, Siriol split into two separate, smaller companies. "[*SuperTed*] did teach us that you can't compete with Disney head on," admits Grace. "We didn't have the material, we didn't have the marketing back up. We burnt our fingers a little bit."

Many of the difficulties facing Siriol and Wales's other independent production companies arise from the international organization of media production and distribution. North American based companies such as Disney and Time Warner are able to operate multinationally, mobilizing resources on a scale beyond the reach of indigenous production companies and broadcasters, and shaping all aspects of the media marketplace.

Whether commissioned by S4C or not, much of the animation made in Wales has been targeted at children's television. The result has been a string of series such as Cartwn Cymru's

Toucan 'Tecs (two toucan detectives) and *Funnybones* (skeletons on the loose), Siriol's *Romuald* (Santa's fun loving reindeer), *The Blobs* (inkblots with colourful personalities) and *Tales of the Tooth Fairies*. After the cancellation of *SuperTed*, S4C's biggest success was *Fireman Sam*. Alongside the work on series, there have also been occasional half hour specials such as Dave Edwards' Siriol Studio's *The Little Engine That Could* and *The Old Man of Lochnagar*. On the face of it, these products have entered an expanding market for children's animation. BBCs One and Two, ITV regional channels, Channel Four and S4C have recently been joined by Fox Kids Network, TCC, The Cartoon Network, Nickelodeon, and the Disney Channel, all of which have animation as a staple diet for children's programming. However, several factors restrict local production companies' access to these markets.

During the 1980s and 1990s, the major film companies in America began acquiring the means of distributing their products. This included ownership of cinemas and cable networks. This is perhaps best exemplified by Time Warner's ownership of Cartoon Network which provides a home for *Scooby-Doo, Wacky Races* and the rest of its recently purchased Hanna-Barbera archive. At the same time, the majors also diversified into other media and acquired ownership or other links with television, video and publishing. Licencing agreements, merchandising and marketing allowed cartoon characters to be exploited across a range of products.

Beyond providing massive resources for further production, ownership of the means of distribution and the mass marketing of properties enable animated cinema films and television programmes to become events, building communities organised around enthusiasm for specific characters and stories. *Hercules* and his cartoon kind can quickly become part of the everyday activities of families, children and their friends via merchandising and licencing agreements that enable the characters to appear in magazines, toy shops and as part of McDonald's Happy Meals. Of course mass marketing cannot guarantee commercial success, but it can be a prerequisite. In terms of television, the pay off is in high ratings. The ratings war between channels can also serve to restrict access to television. The market place for children's animation is highly competitive. Viewing figures are measured every 15 minutes on the BBC. If ratings fall, even an American animated series can find itself removed from the schedules. This was the fate of *Thunder Lizards* on *Live and Kicking*. A more dramatic example was *The Simpsons'* ignominious banishment from Saturday evenings on BBC One to the cult viewing slot on BBC Two.

A final difficulty facing local production is that animation is expensive. Indeed, the expense of animation is one way in which American companies can ensure they engage smaller European companies in a battle which the latter cannot win. It has been estimated that it costs $30 million to get an animation series on US networks. The decisive factor that enables companies in America to bear such costs is their massive home market. But for Time Warner and The Disney Company, television audiences represent only the final market for profit making. Preceeding this, there exists an external market of licencees, who buy the rights to produce products modelled on cartoon characters, and an internal market in which the companies' subsidiaries are encouraged or compelled to trade amongst themselves. It is at this point media conglomerates become like nations themselves, determining the movement of goods within and outside their borders.

Newspaper reports that represent Britain flooded by a tide of cheap American programming are misleading. In Britain, such series are only cheap for television companies that buy the rights to screen second-runs. So if *Rugrats* is less expensive than *Wallace and Gromit* for the BBC to buy, that is partly because the episodes of *Rugrats* will have already been shown on Nickelodeon. Buying these series can also be more cost effective than indigenous production. In Britain, an animated series of 13 episodes of 10 minutes each (a popular format for children's schedules) can cost as much as two million pounds to make. A feature like *Wallace and Gromit: The Wrong Trousers* will cost considerably more.

Britain is a much smaller market than America. Indigenous production companies are therefore dependent on overseas sales and co-production deals that spread the cost of production. Although S4C is heavily funded and committed to local production, its latest commissioning strategy for animation has been formulated to operate in this costly, competitive market. Part of this strategy has been to identify a gap in the market that avoids direct competition with American products. As Naomi Jones, managing director of Cartwn Cymru, says, "You take [a short series for children] to the international marketplace and it just disappears in a sea of animation. S4C have consciously moved to a niche commissioning plan where they knew they were making something nobody else was making so their limited budget could actually make a mark on the world market."

Since then, S4C's policy has commissioned work under the umbrella title of *Animation Classics*, an ambitious series that brings together adaptations of the plays of Shakespeare, operas, religious works and stories such as *The Mabinogion, The Lady of Llyn y Fan Fach* and *Dick Whittington* . Publicity for the project states that *Animation Classics* will have resulted in 72 films and £40 million worth of animation by the millennium. The completed productions have already found an international market, as we indicated earlier.

Animation Classics serves several paymasters and markets. For instance, *Shakespeare – The Animated Tales* was made in association with BBC (Network, Wales, Children's and Education) HIT Entertainment (UK) Home Box Office (USA) and Fujisakei (Japan). For the BBC, *Animation Classics* was able to be screened on BBC 2 as part of that channel's commitment to animation and arts programming and as part of the BBC's educational programming. As well as a shrewd attempt to reposition its product in today's animation marketplace, S4C's latest commissioning strategy has a cultural dimension.

Chris Grace has placed the preservation of cultural heritage in the face of a globalized Disneyfication at the centre of his personal and professional concerns. "I have five kids and I was aware that they were losing a sense of our cultural heritage. The media wasn't helping. It had a disregard for our cultural heritage, unless it was done in the way Disney did it. Frankly what Disney did to *Hunchback* is not the way I would want to do *Hunchback*. They trivialised it. I think you could say that Wales and S4C has been more concerned than most about its own indigenous culture being eroded. That worry is now everywhere."

The 'worry' that an homogenized America is economically and culturally 'everywhere' – the fear of a Mickey Mouse planet – is a symptomatic and defining feature of modern cultural life. In the 1950s, music and comic books from the USA were the focus of these fears, now animation stands accused of eroding national identities by serving as a vehicle for the global spread of a homogenous American culture. Whether distributed as films or television programmes, toys or T-shirts, comics or video cassettes, the products of Walt Disney and Time Warner have become the focus of concerns about the conservation and cultivation of national values and traditions in the face of global corporate interests.

For critics of the global cultural scene, Disney's Mickey Mouse and Donald Duck have become emblems of 'American cultural imperialism.' Disney's more recent creations have also provided cause for concern. The company's attempt to debut *Hercules* in Athens led to heated arguments exemplified by seven pages of articles in *The European* accusing "the quintessential global media corporation of pillaging the central stories through which European nations are represented and imagined: from Victor Hugo's *The Hunchback of Notre Dame* to Hans Anderson's fairy tale of *The Little Mermaid*, described as 'the defining national fable' for Danes."

As yet, the foundational myths and other narratives of Wales and Welshness have rarely been touched by the interests or conventions of The Walt Disney Company. Nevertheless, S4C's *Animation Classics* is explicitly marketed as a response to the Americanisation of the globe. A quotation on the front of one of S4C's publicity brochures reads: "There is a very real and growing fear of a collective loss of memory. The under-exploited resource of animation – boldly and excitingly used, drawing upon the widest available talent – can help address that." It is this felt need to re-work the relationship between past and present, to preserve that which is valued in the present by reasserting a connection with the past and to conserve particular traditions and values of the past in the face of the forgetfulness of global cultural homogenisation, that has turned memory into a site for cultural struggle.

As a commissioning body, S4C can itself be understood as a

response to the feeling that a local language and culture were disappearing. Grace attests, "Wales and S4C have been concerned about [the country's] own indigenous culture being eroded by Anglicisation." But he adds that the cultural heritage the project seeks to preserve is not a specifically Welsh culture. "Once you've animated Shakespeare, you can animate *Moby Dick* as we are doing, you can animate the *Mahabharata*, which is what we intend to do. We are looking at ways of animating the history of the world." Furthermore, this history of the world is intended for transmission around the world.

The belief in universally acceptable products and values is a symptomatic and sometimes necessary part of community building on a global scale. So, the publicity for *Testament – The Bible* in *Animation* notes that "The Bible's influence on the development of many aspects of Western life ... is immeasurable", then moves on to extend this geography by defining the series as "an attempt to underline, for today's audiences, the universal resonances of The Bible and its stories". Links with community building are also explicit. Human beings are storytelling creatures. We tell each other stories in words and music, in pictures, on film, on television and on radio. In these ways we share our experience, reflect our hopes and fears, and develop our shared culture.

Assertions that a product transcends cultural difference are characteristic of the vocabulary of those members of the animation industry who need to reach out across the world and build communities organised around the production, distribution and consumption of their commodities. This vocabulary may best be described as a form of globe-speak. Globe-speak is recognisable by claims that characters, stories, settings and even styles and types of animation are said to have a universal value and appeal.

The simplest, most refined form of globe-speak circulates in the pages of industry magazines such as *Kidscreen* and *Animation International*, at marketing events and in promotional interviews for newspapers. But globe-speak's insistence on transcending cultural difference should not to be confused with talk of Americanisation. The vocabulary of Americanisation is globe speak's pathological counterpart because it bestows national characteristics upon animation in order to regulate against it, to put it in its place. In contrast, globe-speak is utopian.

Globe-speak is one aspect of a very real phenomenon – the transnational spread of animation production, distribution and consumption. Just as the publicity for S4C's *Animation Classics* addresses concerns about local and global culture, so the production of the programmes themselves connects local animation companies to companies and markets around the world. For example, S4C's Shakespeare and *Operavox* series were made primarily by teams of selected ex-Soviet animators working for Christmas Films in Moscow after the dissolution of the Soviet Union.

As S4C has had to engage with the global marketplace, so have those companies in Wales that currently exist beyond its patronage. Single commissions from television companies rarely, if ever, cover the full cost of production. Therefore money has to be raised from selling the rights to distribution in specific territories, advances on sales of ancillary products such as video tapes, private investment from companies or individuals and royalties from character licensing. Behind the cute smiles of Dave Edward's Siriol Animation Studio's *Hot Rod Dogs* can be sensed a desperate urging: "Please turn me into a toy and buy me for Christmas".

After *SuperTed's* cancellation, Siriol Productions began involving itself in the kind of complex business deals that are beginning to characterise the animation industry in Wales. "It was becoming apparent that it was impossible to raise any serious money in one place," recalls Robin Lyons, managing director of Siriol Productions. "We set up a studio grouping with La Fabrique in Montpellier, Sophie Doc in Brussels and Cologne Cartoon. That was called EVA. EVA is now a distribution-exploitation company which the grouping only owns a third of. Most of our work in the last half a dozen years has come through that grouping as co-productions."

Pressure to drive down labour costs is another imperative that has led to connections between animation production in Wales and the rest of the world. Increasingly, manual or semi-skilled tasks such as paint and trace, layout, backgrounds, animation and even storyboarding are being undertaken in countries such as Malaysia and China where wages are significantly lower than even those in Wales.

A paint and trace facility established on the island of La Reunion in the Caribbean reminds us that although animation production is a relative newcomer to the global economic scene, its infrastructure rests upon foundations laid by some of the West's earliest mercantile and colonial adventuring. Not only is labour on La Reunion cheap, the island is also a French territory so companies using its facilities can cash in on trade agreements and co-production benefits. In contrast, S4C's use of studios and animators of the former Soviet Union takes advantage of more recent political restructuring. This can reasonably be represented as an opportunity to open up animation, animators and audiences in the West to the talents and traditions of the East. But there is no question that the crumbling Russian economy has provided a rich vein of skilled but low paid animators.

The development of global production is not inevitable and has not gone unopposed. S4C is not the only source of funding for production in Wales. Training, production, distribution and marketing are supported by *Cartoon*, part of the European Commission's MEDIA initiative. MEDIA, and its successor MEDIA II have supported countries with low production capacity and/or a restricted geographical area, with the ultimate aim of developing "an independent European production and distribution sector".[9] In part, the aim of these initiatives is to redress the six and a quarter billion dollar trade gap in the audio-visual sector between the European Community and the United States.[10]

Once again, the economic issues are coupled with cultural concerns. The European Union seeks to manage the tensions between the cultural specificity of nations and the need to form a European community. Its MEDIA II programme therefore takes into account "the linguistic and cultural diversity of Europe" and "the enhancement of Europe's audio-visual heritage."[11] To this end, it provides support for the training, programme production and initiatives such as Sgrîn, set up to market the products of the Welsh media to the rest of the world.

In this process of localization, the European Union's policy makers sometimes address Europe as a whole, sometimes as individual nations and sometimes as regions within nations. For example *Garlic the Vampire* (fanged fun from producer and director Chris Glynn) was supported by MEDIA's *Cartoon* animation initiative and made mainly in Wales, but at the *Cartoon Forum* at Arles it was listed as a production from the 'United Kingdom.' In fact some of the work on *Garlic* was carried out in France to meet that country's quota system established to preserve culture. So attempts to legislate for the preservation of the local can therefore further globalising tendencies.

Recent international trade agreements can require that a percentage of an animated production is made within national boundaries if the production is to be allowed to be broadcast on that nation's channels. Companies in Wales that are commissioned by other European companies must therefore farm out some of their work to those countries. The aim is to foster the local animation industry while connecting it to a European market that seeks to challenge the American industrial-cultural -entertainment-complex. Of course American companies can play this game too. The Disney Channel has signed deals with French producers such as Gaumont Television, Europe Images and Canal Plus, and sought involvement in local co-productions. There have been tentative attempts to establish US-owned companies in Wales, notably by Hanna-Barbera, though these have met with resistance by some members of the local animation industry concerned that US companies would drain money and siphon talent out of the locale.

Giving animation in Wales a local identity is a complex task because the elements that constitute national and local identities are complex. Identity refers to a set of absolutes such as sameness and unity. But the sameness attributed to national identities can quickly become a series of generalisations that hide important differences. The shared geographies, languages, histories and cultures that are supposed to provide the foundation of nationality are often created, selected, organized and made meaningful in different ways by different people at different places and times.

One way of understanding how the animation industry in Wales puts Wales on the screen would be to examine how the products of that industry depict Wales and Welsh life. Siriol's adaptation of *Under Milk Wood*, Candy Guard's *Pond Life* and even *Fireman Sam* and *Gogs* could then be read as texts to discover the extent to which they represent or fail to represent Welsh life and culture. But this form of analysis would seem to require establishing, *a priori,* those cultural components that could be recognised as essentially Welsh. These might include various selected and invented traditions, canons of literature, customs and languages which form the central or foundational myths through which Wales as a nation is imagined. It would then be possible to praise or castigate members of the animation industry in Wales for succeeding or failing to reproduce this ensemble of essential Welshness: for being stereotypical or not stereotypical enough.

The international market place is one site where national stereotypes are formed. *Brambly Hedge* and Beatrix Potter can be packaged to appeal to overseas expectations, just as holiday brochures present us with countries that are pre-packaged to meet our own clichéd expectations of pleasure. Sales of *Shakespeare – The Animated Tales* to America and Japan can only have been helped by the subject matter's associations with particular definitions of high culture and 'quality' associated with particular constructions of Britishness. As Robin Lyons says "There is this kind of chocolate boxy, picture book expectation, certainly in Japan."

Outside of S4C's *Animated Classics,* other productions from animators working in Wales illustrate the complexity of representing Wales's relationship with America. *Cowboys,* a series of animated shorts by Phil Maloy, re-creates the conventions of the American Western genre, but plays off them in a series of cartoons that make explicit the norms of sexuality and masculinity suppressed by Hollywood. As Maloy says, "If you use the iconography of Hollywood it gives you fantastic freedom so you can create a different kind of universe from the one Cowboys normally operate within. You can say things perhaps that if it was set round where you live wouldn't have the same kind of mythic quality."[12]

Tony Johnson's *Fallen Angels* is an example of the way globalization allows cultures to be constructed and juxtaposed. His futuristic feature, part funded by Fujisakei, is a street-wise mix of 'Japanese' Anime and 'American' film noir. Johnson's work also suggests that people of Wales can adopt hybrid identities, in which previously 'other' cultures are mixed and matched.

From this point of view, an American culture is constructed that can be feared and fun, foreign and familiar. Owain Roberts' student production *Cheesy Dicks* shows how elements of America can be part of Welsh culture. This brief, sexual escapade of a down-at-heel detective can be read as a carnivalesque celebration of the American detective genre and the scatalogical *double-éntendres* of student life. At the same time it sticks two fingers in the face of more polite ways of representing the Welsh language and animation from Wales. Tracy Spottiswoode's *Codename Corgi* (funded by S4C and Sgrîn) is a similarly irreverent take on Welsh identity. It borrows the conventions of the Cold War spy story to toy with stereotypical elements of Welsh culture. The resulting "comi-tragic tale of sex, spies and laverbread" uses Cardiff as a location and manages to play with Wales's relationship with the external world, whilst never losing its sense of place.

Questions of quality and value are often explicit in attempts to preserve and celebrate a country's cultural heritage. To juxtapose *Gerald of Wales* with *Hot Rod Dogs* (and *Kool Kar Kats*), *The Miracle Maker* with Fairwater Film's adaptation of the Viz Comic's *Billy The Fish*, is to juxtapose high culture against low, the sacred against the profane. Grace refers to *Animation Classics'* directors as "auteurs" who each bring their own, personal vision to the classic tale they are contracted to animate. This move opens up a space in which individual creativity can be discussed and contrasted to the demands of marketers, and programme planners who often need a formulaic, industrial product. Defining animation directors as authors also moves *Animation Classics* away from the debased cultural realm occupied by American imports and towards a realm where culture is understood in more prestigious terms as the best that has been thought and said in the world.

The title *Animation Classics* is telling. It is not simply the stories that are being animated that are classics, but the title suggests that these particular adaptations are to be defined as classics of the art of animation. This approach is conservative in that it seeks to preserve the best of the past, but it is too simple to dismiss its particular selection of tradition as the perpetuation of the interests and culture of an elite. Neither can it be said that works such as the Bible are alien to many of the peoples of Wales. Culture is ordinary and it is an ordinary part of cultural life to define and celebrate the extraordinary. Besides which, animation and television as media are often thought too profane to be a vehicle for such celebration. This makes the very idea of animating some of the canonical works of Britain and the world's great traditions seem bold, if not audacious.

Perhaps it is sufficient to celebrate the fact that the animation is in Welsh. After all, it was the struggle to provide access to Welsh that formed the context of Welsh language programming in Wales which led to calls for the formation of S4C. Therefore, one of S4C's primary functions was to contribute to the institutionalisation and administration of language. These functions have informed the commissioning of animation. It was partly S4C's financial support that transformed Joanna Quinn's Beryl, star of *Girls' Night Out* and *Body Beautiful*, from a Mancunian to a bilingual 'valleys girl'.

Discussing the *Animation Classics* project, Grace says, "Everything is possible in the Welsh language. It is the use of language that is important. If it is possible to put *Anna Karenina* into English, it is possible to put it into Welsh as well." But animation, like other kinds of media, offers its own unsettling metaphor by which to understand the relationship between a language and ways of life. In the age of mechanical reproduction, language exists as a sound track that may be removed or added irrespective of the actions, the stories, characters, settings that accompany it. If a Welsh language cannot determine the other types of cultural representation that accompany it, can language be considered the guarantor of a way of life?

There is a place for the approaches outlined above. But a difficulty associated with all of them is that they can lead to a key fallacy that cultures are determined by and reflected in media products. Philip Schlesinger, an academic who has studied the relationship between media policy and cultural identities, has termed this the fallacy of distribution, "according to which it is supposed that distributing the same cultural product leads to an identity of interpretation on the part of those who consume it".[13] Also, from the point of view of production, it would be a fallacy to suggest that the quality of an animated film reflects the quality of life of the animators who made it.

One way in which the animation industry in Wales can be seen to be 'of Wales is in the sense that it shares the economic conditions that characterise Wales. If Wales's animation workforce seems less substantial than older more settled industrial communities, it is partly because the work force is more transient. Industry's need for more flexible, fragmented, patterns of employment means that sometimes there are skills shortages while at other times employers want their workforce to be anywhere other than in their employ.[14]

One way in which the animation industry in Wales differs from the rest of British industry is in the almost complete lack of production work for advertising agencies. This absence is significant, and partly reflects the lack of a commercial culture in Wales capable of sustaining many agencies. That has been changing. However, the economic structures that bring work to Wales and the industries that briefly make their home in Wales also open up Wales to the world.

Global production and consumption lead products and people to flow across national boundaries. So it is not surprising that the animation industry would seem to present us with products that have no place, that do not comfortably "belong" to Wales and appear to threaten its cultural specificity. But this sense of homelessness is not unique to media products and industries in Wales. For instance, it is questionable whether the harbingers of Americanization are actually American at all. Much of the animation on series such as *The Simpsons* is conducted in the Far East and, as economists Colin Hoskins *et al* ask, "did MCA (Universal) change from a US company to a Japanese company and then to a Canadian company when Matsushita bought and then sold its interest to Seagram?"[16]

Raymond Williams, who was born in Wales and who became a founder of cultural studies, argued that the global organization of modern industry shows little respect for nations and that aggressive marketing "flows across nominal frontiers".[17] Williams also rejected the nation as a meaningful source of identity. He did not see himself as a native of Wales, but preferred to locate himself in the familiar environment of his home and local community in the foothills of the Black Mountains. But, like so many claims about the death of nations and nationalisms, Williams' account was premature. The needs of nations are not always the same as the needs of industry. Nations still shape flows and claim allegiances.

Nor is it the case that the global must be in opposition to more personal forms of community. As the managers of animation production companies travel the world, even personal relationships can be globalized. In this and other ways, the global can become familial and inhabit the very home of nativity. But to suggest animation in Wales is a global enterprise is to again fall prey to the allure of globe-speak. Conditions of production are as specific as places such as towns, cities or regions, so it is necessary to note which parts of the world are utilised in which aspects of production.

Even though the Welsh animation scene has steadily grown since the early 1980s, it still does not possess the infrastructure or the skills base necessary to support a substantial industry capable of effectively competing with the likes of Disney on a global scale. And it never will. Therefore S4C and the European Commission still have a vital role to play in supporting Welsh animation. Just how tenuous the industry is, can be judged by the recent departure of Dave Edwards to America and the collapse of Aaargh Animation. But economic pressure can be productive; 1999 saw the establishment of the Welsh Animation Group (WAG) partly set up to lobby the British government for the same kind of tax breaks enjoyed by animation companies in the rest of Europe.

Interestingly, WAG places Welsh animation in a British context and sees the difficulties facing local animation as problems for animation production in Britain as a whole. This again raises questions about cultural specificity of animation in Wales. But, before anyone complains that the animation industry in Wales is not Welsh enough, it is useful to recall that attempts to establish national production can rest on sets of stereotypical assumptions about a nation in which the diversity of its peoples is lost.

Historian Gwyn A. Williams provided a different way of thinking about national production when he wrote "Wales is an artefact which the Welsh produce", and suggested that the Welsh make and remake Wales day by day, year by year, generation after generation "if they want to".[18] Of course there is a need to define who are "the Welsh" but one advantage of Williams' perspective is that Wales and Welshness cannot be seen as over and done with – a finished product – but as projects that are still in development. If animation is to be seen as part of that production, what needs to be asked is: who will own the means of production? Who will take part in the process of production? And who will feel a sense of ownership of the product?

Notes

We thank the members of the animation industry for their time in talking to us, also Donovan Keogh for arranging and conducting some of the interviews on which this chapter is based, and Martin Barker, Matthew Hills, Brian Fagence, Hugh Mackay and Deborah Painting for their comments and corrections. This work derives from research funded by the European Commission's Information Society Project Office.

Notes

1. See Meehan's account of the structure of ownership and control behind the Batman movie. Eileen Meehan 'Holy Commodity Fetish, Batman!: The Political Economy of a Commercial Intertext', in Roberta E. Pearson and William Uriccho (eds), *The Many Lives of The Batman: Critical Approaches to a Superhero and his Media* (London: Routledge, 1991).
2. Interview with Naomi Jones, conducted by Donovan Keogh and Tim Robins, 3 April, 1997.
3. See Ariel Dorfman and Armand Mattelart, *How to Read Donald Duck: Imperialist Ideology in the Disney Comic*, (New York: International General, 1984) [Second Edition] . This marxist propaganda account analyses Disney comics as an example of American Imperialism. The continued use of Mickey Mouse as an emblem for American global culture is noted by Kevin Robins, 'What in the World's Going On?', in Paul du Gay (ed) *Production of Culture/Cultural Production* (London: Sage, 1997).
4. *The European*, 381, 28th August-3rd September 1997, pp.5-12.
5. Disney's *The Black Cauldron* being a notable exception.
6. Over the last two decades, there has been an increasing interest in the role memory plays in the construction of identity. Simply put, who we think we are can depend on knowing who we have been. Identity implies a continuity over time. A number of groups have sought to question how the relationship between the past and the present is constructed. See, for example, Richard Johnson, Gregor McLennan, Bill Schwarz and David Sutton (eds), *Making*

Histories: Studies in History-writing and Politics (London: Hutchinson, 1982). Such accounts have questioned the way heritage industries construct accounts of history that marginalize or silence the experiences and interests of particular groups, for example, the working class. More recently, memory has also been seen as a nostalgic attempt to create a sense of place, home and country in the face of the decline of national cultures. See Erica Carter, James Donald & Judith Squires (eds), *Space & Place: Theories of Identity and Location* (Lawrence & Wishart: London, 1993).

7. Angharad Tomos, 'Realising a Dream', and Jonathan Coe, 'Sianel Pedwar Cymru – Fighting for a Future', both in Simon Blanchard and David Morley (eds), *What's this Channel Fo(u)r? An Alternative Report* (Comedia: London, 1982).

8. Interview with Robin Lyons, conducted by Tim Robins, 18 June, 1997.

9. *Ibid.*

10. *Media,* 15 June, 1997, p.3.

11. *MEDIA II: A Programme of the European Union,* p.l.

12. Interview with Phil Maloy, conducted by Andy Cole, Ieuan Morris, Tim Robins and Chris Webster, 7 July, 1997.

13. Philip Schlesinger. 'Wishful thinking: cultural politics, media and collective identities in Europe', in Annabella Sreberny-Mohammadi, Dwayne Winseck, Jim McKenna and Oliver Boyd-Barrett (eds), *Media in Global Context: a Reader* (Arnold: London, 1997) p.73.

14. The recent Skillset report on employment in the animation industry notes that 24% of respondents were employed on a contract of unspecified length or on a freelance basis (Myra Woolf, Alan Chisnall and Sara Holly, *The Animation Industry* 1997/98, [Skillset: London]). However, the type of work undertaken (e.g. in-betweening) can determine the type of contract and in Wales the percentage of animators on short term contracts or working freelance may be much higher.

15. Myra Woolf, Alan Chisnall and Sara Holly, *The Animation Industry* 1997/98, (Skillset: London). 101 companies in England and Wales reported that 38 per cent of the companies produced animation for commercials. The population was estimated at approximately 300 companies in England and Wales, employing 3000 individuals.

16. Colin Hoskins, Stuart McFadyen and Adam Finn, *Global Television and Film: an Introduction to the Economics of the Business* (Clarendon Press: Oxford, 1997) p.37.

17. Raymond Williams, 'The Culture of Nations', *Towards 2000* (Chatto & Windus, The Hogarth Press: London, 1983) p.189.

18. Gwyn A. Williams, *When Was Wales? A History of the Welsh,* (London: Black Raven Press, 1985) p.304.

Unearthing the Present:
Television Drama in Wales
Dave Berry

The resignation of Karl Francis as BBC Wales drama head in May 1997 was symptomatic of the problems and malaise affecting English-language TV plays and movies in Wales for most of the previous two decades.

Even the discovery of new Welsh language writing talent, and the gradual, encouraging metamorphosis of S4C drama – from the days of its undue emphasis on period 'rural and folkloric' dramas in the early 1980s to the stress on contemporary work by current drama commissioner Angharad Jones – fails to compensate for the dearth of credible English language feature length drama emerging from Wales. The lack of opportunities for monolingual (or Anglo-Welsh) writers and directors, in particular, should continue to cause grave concern.

The disparity between television opportunities in Welsh and English language drama, with the balance firmly in favour of generally seriously underfunded Welsh language work, continues to retard English language writing – and crucially affect confidence and self-esteem in Wales. Even the more ambitious Welsh language TV dramas, when earmarked for cinema release, have tended to be scuppered by timorous London distributors and agents, who lack confidence in the marketing potential of 'subtitled' movies (at least from nations lacking a *film tradition*). It's plainly scandalous that *Hedd Wyn* (1992) Oscar-nominated and winner of the Royal Television Society Best Drama award has failed to gain distribution in England. Endaf Emlyn's 1995 feature drama *Y Mapiwr* / The Making of Maps (1995) was effectively dropped by London-based agents The Sales Company, and has still not gained widespread British release – despite fine critical reviews from the feature's London

Film Festival screening, and Emlyn's own reputation rose after *Gadael Lenin* (1993) landed the Best British Film audience prize at the LFF.

English language drama in Wales was at a low ebb when Francis, the best known and most prolific Welsh film director since the 1970s, arrived at BBC Wales HQ in Llandaff, Cardiff, in January 1996 with an impeccable radical pedigree. It seemed to augur well for his relationship with the left-wing historian Dai Smith, head of BBC Wales English language broadcasting, who established his academic credentials to a wider world as co-author of *The Fed* (the history of the South Wales Miners' Federation) and writer of the Welsh Rugby Union official history *Field of Dreams*. Here at last, some more gullible pundits thought, was a BBC Wales pairing promising strong, committed indigenous work albeit, perhaps, with a southern valleys bias and of the social realist stamp which had characterised Smith's writings and Francis's films from *Above Us The Earth* (1976) to *Streetlife* (1995).

In *Streetlife*, a harrowing if overheated BBC Screen Two study of a jilted single mother driven to infanticide on a South Wales council estate rife with drugs and prostitution, Francis had shown what might be done with 'English' drama in Wales. Written during his brief previous tenure as BBC Wales executive in charge of special projects (a virtual sinecure as it turns out – given the cash drought for productions) the drama seemed, in retrospect, to set his stall out and point the way forward. Yet the seeds of mistrust were in *Streetlife's* genesis and its pre-production problems hinted, in microcosm, at the schism between a metrocentric broadcasting bureaucracy and the BBC Wales drama department – notably conspicuous by its lengthy absences from the network after the early 'eighties.

For George Faber, then the head of BBC single dramas in London, was not noticeably smitten with Francis's own script. He gave his consent to the project only after an impassioned plea from the then BBC Wales drama head Ruth Caleb, who believed strongly in the project's potential.

Even then Faber insisted that the budget, finally between £310,000 and £350,000, should be well below the cost of other (generally English based and originated) dramas in the slot, virtually forcing Francis to cut corners in a six-week shoot. Despite the constraints, the film garnered extravagant paeans of praise following its enthusiastic reception at the Edinburgh Film Festival where it was championed by the event's director, Mark Cousins. The film (which also delighted a chastened Faber) gained much from the strong central performance Francis coaxed from Helen McCrory, though it suffered from the director's familiar scattergun approach to social and political problems. The critical success finally prompted a tardy BBC decision to blow the film up from 16mm to 35mm, primarily for international festival release and overseas sales.

Streetlife gave the impression that Francis would lead from the front. There were healthy signs during his sojourn's early days. Hundreds of actors, technicians and would-be directors filed into BBC Llandaff one day, early in his regime, to hear the director's clarion call for more relevant contemporary indigenous product and his intention to give jobs to home-based talent rather than to Welsh exiles in London (despite his earlier choice of McCrory, a London-based stage actress with Welsh roots who had never worked in Wales). Francis also startled insiders by initiating a series of workshops organised by two character actors, Gary Howe and Roger Knott, who had been peripheral to in-house drama, but were, significantly, alumni of the director's own films. It was clear Francis sought to shake up thinking in a department he considered stale and hidebound by tradition and too prone to comply passively with the status quo (e.g. the acceptance of London judgements of their product's suitability for the network). He had also been critical of a predominance of the Welsh language establishment in the higher echelons of BBC Wales since the 1970s, which he felt militated against a strong commitment to English language work. Francis thought it vital for Welsh drama's credibility that he build up, with London, a roster of "bankable Welsh actors". The Polygram release *Twin Town*, for all its faults, showed that we have actors of real class – Rhys Ifans, Dorien Thomas, Sue Roderick, etc. Francis wanted to broaden the base of talent and improve acting standards, and he inveighed against the alleged inertia or compromises of the regimes of the two previous drama heads, John Hefin and Ruth Caleb.

Eighteen months later optimism had drained away. Francis departed after achieving comparatively little, though Howe's long-term contribution in increasing the pool of Welsh actors auditioning for roles should not be underestimated. Francis left complaining (like his predecessors) of the BBC's alleged intractability and intransigence and lack of faith in Welsh-initiated projects and felt his artistic ability was being strangled by the bureaucracy and London's lack of faith in his ideas. Francis had been anxious to dramatise numerous works by the great Welsh novelist-playwright Gwyn Thomas, for example, and to realise a pet project, an Elaine Morgan script, *Rage*, the Caitlin Thomas-Dylan Thomas story.

Francis was swiftly disheartened by the low budgets for indigenous work generally, and London's tendency to override his wishes on drama priorities and nominate films with what he saw as only tenuous Welsh connections to 'leapfrog' the dramas on his own priority list. Francis found his own track record availed little, faced with what London regarded as a decade of disappointing Welsh products and it was also soon obvious that Smith, elevated to his TV post largely on the strength of radio work as producer and presenter, lacked the clout to influence the bureaucrats. The writing was on the wall when Francis fired off a desperate – and predictably fruitless – memo (until now kept entirely under wraps), asking Michael Jackson, in effect to put his money where his mouth was (in professing BBC support for more regional drama) by ploughing £6 million into Welsh drama over two years.[1]

Francis had encountered the kind of problems that had blighted the performances of both Caleb and Hefin. Before his arrival BBC Wales had launched pre-production work on *Harper and Iles* (1996), a two-part pilot for a projected but aborted police series, directed by an Englishman Jim Hill and written by the South Wales novelist and journalist James Tucker (under his Bill James pseudonym). The dramas effectively introduced as a lead actor Aneurin Hughes – later seen to more advantage in Ceri Sherlock's 1997 S4C drama *Cameleon* (Chameleon) – but failed to gain the nod from the BBC hierarchy, perhaps because, in order to make the necessary impact quickly, planned future episodes had been yoked together hurriedly. The two parts screened also lacked any strong local identity – the urban Wales presented in *Harper and Iles* seemed distinctly nebulous. It was a familiar tale.

Prior to S4C's launch, and later after the launch, arguably too much of the BBC Wales drama budget was diverted to the long-running soap *Pobol y Cwm* (People of the Valley), launched in 1974, though BBC had also attempted a police thriller genre series *Bowen a'i Bartner* (1984-88) – set enterprisingly and unusually in Cardiff, and written by Sion Eirian, past winner of the Welsh Eisteddfod Crown and co-writer of Endaf Emlyn's feature *Gadael Lenin* (1993).

By the mid-eighties a chorus of dissenting voices criticised the dearth of English language single and multi-episode dramas compared with the situation in the '60s and '70s. There were no English language writers being developed to match the stature, in Welsh, of the north Walians Rhydderch Jones and Gwenlyn Parry – in-house BBC stalwarts (as producer and script editor, respectively). The pair, co-writers of one of the most popular of all Welsh TV series *Fo a Fe*, were regularly commissioned for Welsh language work.

BBC Wales drama head John Hefin, accused in some quarters of favouring Welsh, tried to plug the perceived gaps in English and there was a brief flowering of committed social dramas, set in both past and present. The most interesting included *Penyberth* (1985, dir. Peter Edwards) about the infamous 1936 Welsh nationalists' raid and arson at an RAF station in the Llyn Peninsula – an incident which earned notoriety for Plaid leader Saunders Lewis – and *The Mimosa Boys* (1985, dir. John Hefin) which implied British government culpability for the Gallahad tragedy in the Falklands war. Richard Lewis's *Babylon Bypassed* (1998) may have been wildly uneven and blighted by specious special effects, but Meic Povey's script conveyed, through the ruminations of a failed thespian and his protégé, the Welsh sense of loss and confusion in the post-industrial era. It was centred on a community breaking up and literally split by a motorway (shades of the Marc Evans/Ed Thomas drama documentary *Pentre Mud* (Silent Village) (1995) set in the playwright's native Cwmgiedd). These plays at least dealt intriguingly with aspects of the language and culture, and suggested, fascinatingly, the threat (and the temptations) imposed on Welsh communities by outsiders.

Francis had been concerned that, under Caleb, little work of relevance to Wales had emerged and too much emphasis had been placed on outside directors and actors for supposedly Welsh productions, with London-based Tristram Powell, for example, directing a version of the Kingsley Amis novel *The Old Devils*, the dramatised Gwyn Thomas autobiography *Selected Exits* (1993) and the 1994 *Oliver's Travels* (with Alan Bates in the lead) – written by another 'outsider', Alan Plater. Francis was also concerned about the casting of the English actor Kevin Whately in the 'showy' role of the wife-beating school head in *Trip Trap* (1996) in preference to Welsh actors, just as Chris Menges had been pressured to take a box office actor, (William Hurt, eventually) rather than his first choice, Welshman Owen Teale, for his Borders cinema feature *Second Best* (1995).

Francis and Caleb have both also stressed the debilitating effects on Welsh drama of London's similar unwillingness to invest in Welsh writing talent – other than 'established' names like Andrew Davies, and the veteran Ewart Alexander who gained credibility (like Elaine Morgan) in the comparatively early days of television when the main London-based television channels were more receptive to outsiders. In the 'fifties and 'sixties there was a plethora of drama – albeit mainly versions of the classics or work from such old-fashioned Welsh dramatists as the north Walian screen and stage star Emlyn Williams or south Wales comedy writer and populist Eynon Evans. The period in the 'sixties when the BBC boasted four drama producers – David Thomas, Dafyd Gruffydd, Emyr Humphreys and George Owen may not necessarily have broken down many creative barriers, but their sojourn seems a Golden Age compared to most of the years since, as one respected current writer, Meic Povey, has acknowledged.

Wales may not have a surfeit of writing talent – but it does harbour a clutch of writers with good track records, notably Ed Thomas, Steve Gough, Meic Povey, Alun Richards and the Brookside writer Peter Cox. Most of these writers have produced works presenting ordinary lives and experiences, and encouraging viewers to identify with characters and situations.

Yet Francis's arrival coincided with a drought in BBC productions for network. BBC Wales had already initiated the eight part series (or 'soap') *Tiger Bay*, though Francis soon took over the reins as executive producer and called in, as consultant, Welsh-born Pedr James (co-director of the successful BBC networked series *Our Friends in the North* and soon-to-be Francis's successor in the BBC Wales drama hot seat). Again, the apparent wish to please London led to compromise (and an English director, Ian White). Early episodes gained a lacklustre critical response and the programme failed to impart any real indigenous flavour. Despite its welcome foregrounding of black actors previously long ignored by BBC Wales – after a trawl which involved auditioning more than 450 actors – the series had little Welsh flavour, partly because the chosen locale, the Cardiff docks (now being gentrified as 'the Bay'), has no real identity. Perhaps more pertinently, there was little sense in *Tiger Bay* of a multilingual docks culture. The ethnicity had, it seemed, been laundered to suit BBC expectations and the network slot.

During his spell as Llandaff drama head, Francis initiated the odd feature and half-hour drama from new talent, but few of these ventures reached the screen. One or two works were in the late 'nineties being developed as spin-offs from an aborted 'city project', a planned Cardiff-based portmanteau thriller-feature laden with black humour in which four directors and five writers experimented with form and fed stories into one overall movie. The project, always low key and low priority within BBC Wales, was mooted in its early days as a possible model in pointing new directions for experimental drama throughout Britain, but it foundered after a 16 month gestation, ostensibly because BBC Wales considered the material for the intrinsic stories too disparate.[2]

The four series of BBC Playhouse thirty-minute dramas designed to encourage new talent were hamstrung, and betrayed by, their penny-pinching budgets (£150,000-£200,000 a series). The cost-cutting, unimaginative content, and some lethargic direction and lamentable shot selection, suggested a fatal lack of confidence and guidance (exceptions were Giancarlo Gemin's *Broken Glass* (1993) and Phil John's *Moniker* (1995). The work, generally, was rarely more impressive than the two Shot in a Shoebox series, each featuring several 15-minute shorts by students, which threw up some work of promise – despite the derisory total budget for each series of £20,000.[3]

Even delight in the 'nineties student 'discoveries' such as Michael Barnes's *Joy Ride* and Jon Jones's *Rouble*, for example, was tempered by the realisation that they were 'bought in' works and the BBC had made no investment in their development.

After leaving his post, Francis claimed to have inherited a legacy of 'contempt', felt by London paymasters towards the BBC Wales drama department – an attitude he uncharitably if understandably attributed, in part, to the failure of successive previous script editors and drama heads here to nurture new writing or directing talent.

Francis deserves a modicum of credit for developing some fresh talent, notably through the 1996-97 PICS scriptwriting scheme, a joint venture from BBC Wales and the then Wales Film Council (resulting in four very different 10-minute shorts targeted at theatrical release). The movies, which earned much praise at the Edinburgh Film Festival, seemed bound to cause a ripple in TV viewings at least and contained highly atmospheric works of rare merit. *The Confectioner* was a personal, almost abstract feminist work centred on sexual power play and repression, with form and content superbly married by the director Margaret Constantas and photographer Phil Cowan; and *Birdbrain*, a psychological murder thriller from a script by Welsh stage writer Greg Cullen was notable for its striking imagery and Eric Styles's confident direction. *Horse City*, directed by Catrin Clarke, contained images of real power and gained Clarke a place among fourteen British short films selected for showcasing on BBC's *The Talent*.

Despite these odd minor successes, Francis gave himself no time to do better than Hefin – or Caleb, whose spell was characterised by dramas which may have satisfied London but led to widespread disenchantment in Wales, as they relied so heavily on outsiders (lead actors, directors and writers). *Tender Loving Care* (1993), centred on a murderous nurse with a penchant for euthanasia, won awards from BAFTA Cymru and was directed by north Walian Dewi Humphreys, son of writer and sometime television producer Emyr – but its leads Dawn French and Rosemary Leach, and writer Lucy Gannon were all from England. *Trip Trap* (1996), undoubtedly an impressive, disturbing work was again scripted by Gannon and directed by another outsider, Danny

Hiller; and *Cormorant* (1993), an assured study of a marital rela-
tionship scarred by the husband's obsession and a bird's alien
presence, had an English director Peter Markham and starred
Ralph Fiennes. These credits make chastening reading and the
dramas were scarcely more Welsh than the 1986-87 trio of dramas
from the London-based team of David Stone (director), David M.
Thompson (producer) and William Nicholson (writer) – *The
Vision*, with Dirk Bogarde and Lee Remick, *Shadowlands* (with
Joss Ackland and Claire Bloom), and *New World*, (starring
Bernard Hill and James Fox). These three dramas were shot in
Wales but the BBC at Llandaff, despite gaining reflected glory, did
little more than crew up the productions.[4]

Even *Filipina Dreamgirls* (1991), an amusing study of a
motley group of Welshmen hunting for wives in the Philippines
which gained much from Andrew Davies's colourful character-
isations (from Ray Gravell's mother's boy to David Thewliss's
comically vacuous, swaggering wide boy and sexual fantasist)
was directed by Salford's Les Blair. (The situation in English
language drama in Wales in the mid-nineties, with many film-
makers and much acting talent imported, provided an odd echo
of the Welsh language situation in S4C's first year. Faint
hearted executives of the Welsh Fourth Channel at that time
decided – inexplicably – that an outsider, Yorkshireman James
Hill, should direct *Owain Glyndwr* (Owen Glendower) (1983),
rather than indigenous directors, such as Wil Aaron and Alan
Clayton, steeped in Welsh language culture.[5]

Ruth Caleb during her BBC Wales stay, spoke of deplorable
funding with BBC Wales producing no more than two network
dramas a year at £600,000 each.[6] Her decision to opt for so
much work with non-Welsh creative and acting involvement
smacked of the line of least resistance. The one Welsh director
to emerge from this period was Marc Evans (later to direct
perhaps the most powerful of all Welsh big screen dramas,
House of America). Evans, with the BBC Wales drama series
Friday On My Mind (1992), with Chris Eccleston and Maggie
O'Neill and *Thicker Than Water* (1993), featuring Jonathan
Pryce and Theresa Russell, produced works with a significant
emotional charge. He revealed a strong cinematic flair and
sensibility, using locations with ingenuity – notably the bleak

Cardiff docks wasteland, mirroring the lead male character's state of mind in *Thicker Than Water*. *Friday On My Mind* was, incidentally, the first independent drama from BBC Wales under the new 25 percent 'indie' quota regulations. *House of America*, with a superb script from Ed Thomas, re-working his stage drama, called for a Wales woefully lacking in self-confidence to develop – or invent – its own contemporary mythology. It explored a west Wales valleys community subsumed by American industry and transatlantic culture – chiefly through characters finally demented by their obsession with ubiquitous American mythology. BBC London, fairly typically, turned down the script, and the film could only be made after a few more drafts and after Sheryl Crown, then a BBC producer, left and took the project to London's September Films. The treatment of Evans and Thomas by the Beeb, centrally, recalled its refusal to up the ante and invest more than originally projected in Welsh director Chris Monger's *The Englishman Who Went Up A Hill, But Came Down A Mountain* (1994), commissioned by Caleb. It was finally backed by the powerful US-based Miramax to the tune of a mere £5 million, and grossed double its costs in the first month of US theatrical release.

The BBC London drama hierarchy's reluctance to support and develop Welsh work certainly suggests an inherent prejudice. Even Marc Evans' BBC Wales 'nineties dramas couldn't conceal the overall paucity of opportunities for emerging indigenous talent – especially in English, hence the frequent calls over the years for a fifth Welsh channel in English and the spawning in the 'nineties of a new pressure group, the Campaign for Welsh Television in the English Language.

The roots of the problem lie deep. As Alan Clayton, former Welsh film director and ex-HTV Wales drama head, said recently – "For years, there has been a marked lack of self-belief in Welsh writing and directing talent both in Wales and London. There is a perception within Wales that works deriving from Wales won't be sexy enough in London. This feeling has led to compromise and apathy." The sentiments are shared by Meic Povey who believes that "there's far too much looking over one's shoulder towards London seeking approval. It's bound to lead to the compromises we've seen in the casting of the series *Lifeboat*

(1994) and *Drover's Gold* (1997), for example. We would be much better off now bringing on talent, developing skills for domestic consumption in the first place."

You might have sympathy for this view and for Ealing's renowned producer Michael Balcon's perceptive tenet that to do fine international work, you must first do good national work. But, clearly, any official BBC Wales reluctance to seek network slots for its talent would be untenable given the overheads in Llandaff. In the meantime, more Welsh producers and directors share the disenchantment of Paul Turner, who believes that "Wales is still treated as a colonial outpost by London".[7]

Since Francis's resignation, BBC Wales has continued to under-perform, producing little of intrinsic merit. Trevor Griffiths, a writer of innate radical sympathies, was invited to direct his own script for *Food for Ravens*, a misbegotten slice of wispish, inchoate whimsy commissioned by Dai Smith in which an acidic Nye Bevan (Brian Cox) reflected from his death bed, on his life and the temper of politics over the decades. The film was intended to strike a cautionary note in the era of New Labour and to fire a warning shot across the bows of a party drifting inexorably rightwards but seemed simplistic and irritatingly schematic, reducing Bevan in stature as it skittered over crucial political issues. Cox's public statements about alleged BBC exec-utive bias against the programme (and by inference the drama department at Llandaff), following London's apparent initial reluctance to network *Food for Ravens,* rang hollow given the slightness and vapidity of the piece.

Just as problematic and disappointing was another Smith commission, which appeared under the Arts and Music rather than Drama department banner. Michael Bogdanov had directed a wildly uneven but at times invigorating version of *The Tempest* in Cardiff's docklands. His follow up, *Light in The Valley* (1998), part of a projected trilogy on Welsh life, centred on the south Wales coalfield and explored the notion of communal memory impinging on the present, and seemed intended as a partial critique of an amnesiac or demoralised community alienated from its radical past. The work fell awkwardly between drama and documentary and amounted to an ill-conceived primer. Bogdanov's every touch betrayed his lack of genuine insight and his 'outsider's' perspective which rendered most of his attempts to discuss stereotyping and the accretions of the past as patronising and platitudinous.

More encouraging were the shorts and one work in particular, the genial, humane comedy *Washed Up* (1998) directed by Eric Styles and written by Steve Gough – a drama rooted in under-standing of character and loving observation of individual foibles. It confirmed the potential of Gough, whose *Heartland* about a west Wales farmer facing bankruptcy due to the EEC butter market and regulations, attracted Anthony Hopkins to the main role. Hopkins, increasingly committed to Wales after a forlorn career hiatus in Hollywood, was also impressive as the writer Gwyn Thomas in *Selected Exits*.

Yet at the end of the 'nineties, there were still no clear signs of either a policy for drama in BBC Wales, or a body of national work emerging. At least the BBC has occasionally supplied work relevant to both past and present. HTV have, all too often since landing the franchise in 1968, abrogated their responsibilities towards drama in Wales, providing pitifully thin budgets to do worthwhile work. There were a few flickerings of life in the 'eighties and Alan Clayton, former head of HTV Wales drama, directed two of the finest Welsh small screen works of the past decade or so – *Better Days* (1988) and *Ballroom* (1988-89), from scripts by south Walian valleys writer Robert Pugh, better known as an actor. The first centred on a widowed former miner (Glyn Houston), dislocated when torn from his valleys roots to live with his incompatible, social climbing son in a Porthcawl suburb. The other was a robust slice of valleys life, remarkable for its occasionally ribald but always authentic humour, colourful colloquialisms, painful and volatile recrimi-nations and strong (not to say) overbearing female roles. It also explored with great intelligence the clash of loyalty to roots and cultural aspirations facing a valleys man exposed to the wider world by education. These tensions were teased out in Pugh's script, which suffered little in comparison with the Welsh cinema films similarly concerned with the impact and trans-forming powers of education on individual working men (the 1945 and 1979 cinema versions of *The Corn is Green*, and Jill Craigie's 1949 *Blue Scar*, for example). The success of both

Clayton dramas owed much to Pugh's feeling for dialogue and character and to the creators' affinity with their protagonists' experience – Pugh as a product of the valleys and Clayton as a miner's son from the Wrexham area. Clayton also directed *Old Scores* (1991), an HTV co-production with New Zealand, playing on the Welsh passion for rugby union and a work similar on flavour to John Hefin's highly popular BBC Wales comedy *Grand Slam* (1978), which featured Hugh Griffith, Windsor Davies *et al,* as reprobates in Paris for the big match and seeking earthy distractions. Clayton has always felt *Ballroom* and *Better Days* were the most satisfying work of his career, and in 1997 he was back directing, with *Hen Elynion* (Old Enemies), an S4C drama set in his native north east Wales, with a mainly amateur cast from the same area and loosely based on the miner and heroic Spanish Civil War prisoner Tom Jones.

HTV's record in supporting indigenous drama through most of the 'nineties has been even more distressing than the BBC's – despite Clayton and Pugh's spectacular audience coup earlier with the first series of *We Are Seven* (1988), a throwback to the channel's bucolic period dramas, transplanting an Irish tale to rural Wales. The episodes at least were suffused with warmth and humour (in the *Only Two Can Play* vein), providing a showcase for Welsh actors in meaty, distinctive roles. In producing *Ballroom* and *Better Days* in the 'eighties, work deriving strength from everyday situations, HTV had responded to the IBA's expressed disappointment about the huge preponderance of Bristol-based drama in HTV schedules. Around that time HTV Wales was guaranteed around 11 hours of network drama a year but a shake-up of independent television's structure took away the guarantee and left the channel pitching against the big guns in a market increasingly driven by audience ratings.

Clayton believed that indigenous drama by writers with feet in the community gave credence to the argument that 'back yard speaks to back yard' and working class dramas of ordinary experience could succeed with a wider audience.[8] Scotland, significantly, succeeded with *Taggart* and *Tutti Frutti* in producing material very specific to its own locales and culture but also able to disarm and enthuse viewers elsewhere, thanks to the original writing, sharp characterisation and local vernacular.

In 1993 HTV did produce a fine three-part police thriller, *Tell Tale*, written with style and wit by Ewart Alexander, but, strangely, Pugh himself has never written for television since the early 'nineties (a huge indictment of HTV), and the channel has soaked up drama budgets in such dubious exercises as recording series of plays at the Sherman Theatre, Cardiff. These have, generally, been creatively moribund, and even more recent attempts to open out the Sherman material beyond constricting time format and studio settings have resulted in embarrassing work. Until recently, HTV has failed English language drama in Wales miserably and you can't help wondering at the sheer failure of imagination which prevented the channel even trying to develop, beyond its half-hour straitjacket, a work as intrinsically potent and harrowing as Michael Bogdanov's *Break, My Heart*, one of the 1997 Sherman Plays, culled from a stage drama by the now Welsh based Arnold Wesker and already a *cause célèbre* in the theatre.

The arrival at HTV of a new drama head Peter Edwards, a prolific producer and director for Cardiff production company Lluniau Lliw, seemed to herald some hope of increasing commitment to home-grown drama at a time of renewed expectation in Wales with the launch of the Welsh Assembly. Edwards's first major commission was a three part thriller *In The Company of Strangers* (1999), set against a backdrop of political skulduggery in and around the Assembly, directed by Endaf Emlyn, his first contemporary genre film outside comedy (and longest work in English), from a script by Rob Gittings and Wil Roberts. Edwards, also instigated an energetic if raw 'working class' serial or 'soap', *Nuts and Bolts*, from a script by Merthyr's Lynnette Jenkins, an M.A. graduate of the University of Glamorgan. In what seemed another bold move, Edwards invited ideas from the valleys and mixed amateur and professional actors in pre-serial acting workshop sessions in the quest for authenticity. The series was transmitted in 1999.

The sojourn at HTV in the mid-nineties of Geraint Morris, an experienced series producer, as a drama adviser had achieved some small impact – it led directly to the emergence of Tylorstown writer John Owen as a distinctive new voice, supplying HTV dramas to S4C. Morris – who died in 1997 – was a huge inspiration on the former teacher, taking him through draft after draft refining the work. The relationship demonstrated the value of creative producers (singularly lacking in Wales according to Euryn Ogwen Williams, S4C's former programme controller).[9] The result was two engrossing single-dramas, and a series. Owen's most challenging and best work, *Yn Gymysg Oll I Gyd* (All Mixed Up), homed in with great force and integrity on the problem of schizophrenia and its impact on the sufferer, a talented extrovert teacher (Richard Elfyn) and, particularly, his doting, increasingly depressed wife. Owen performed a dextrous balancing act, eliciting audience sympathy for the couple during terrifying scenes in which she cajoled and humoured her spouse (much given to poetic flights of fancy, fierce jealousy and crushing, sardonic observations) and fought to hold together a disintegrating marriage during his switchback mood changes. At times these emotional swings seemed too sudden and Elfyn's perkiness, during moments of rationality, a little forced – but the film was written with sensitivity and earmarked director Eric Styles as a considerable 'discovery'. Styles was later to direct the flawed cinema feature, *Dreaming of Joseph Lees*.

Owen's other HTV work for S4C was Terry Dyddgen Jones's *Bydd Yn Wrol* (Be Brave), a lighter affair, centering on a Rhondda community finding common ground and solidarity in a battle to save a village centre from the maw of developers. Owen's rather broad comedy suffered from an uneven tone, but was essentially optimistic, displaying a genuine feel for the idioms of his native area, and was, of course, similar in theme to Stephen Bayly's 1986 *Coming Up Roses* (Rhosyn a Rhith), the 1999 Welsh cinema comedy house and the comedies of Ealing's forties heyday. It presented a local community burying domestic disputes to thwart importunate outsiders and money men. The film had a more serious undercurrent, with Owen exploring the inner tumult of a worried homosexual (Matthew Rhys) considering the implications of 'coming out'. Owen emulated Endaf Emlyn and Sion Eirian in their script for *Gadael Lenin* (Leaving Lenin), in exploring sensitive issues of sexual gender in a humorous context while never diminishing, or parodying, his characters' needs or dilemmas.

The stress in S4C's early days was on costume pieces or rural period one-off series or dramas (*Owain Glyndŵr, Madam Wen,*

Joni Jones, Wil Six, and any number of period Teliesyn dramas and drama-docs from Paul Turner – and also Colin Thomas, whose political films, made with the bellicose sometime Marxist historian Gwyn Alf Williams, often admittedly had great contemporary resonance). In recent years the channel has at last begun to pay its dues to the present and its concerns.

Crucial in changing the emphasis to more modern subjects were Karl Francis's *Boy Soldier* (Milwr Bychan) (1986), a study of a valley boy's ambivalent feelings serving with the British army in northern Ireland, and, even more significantly, his *Yr Alcoholig Llon* (The Happy Alcoholic). This 1984 study of marital break up and one man's battle against his obsession, gained credibility from Francis's own experiences as an avowed alcoholic in his earlier career. Just as significant was *Coming Up Roses* and Bayly, significantly, levelled the 'folkloric' and 'bucolic' allegations against S4C as early as the late 'eighties.[10] This fundamentally gentle but occasionally trenchant comedy used the closure of a cinema as a metaphor for urban blight and pit closures under Thatcherism. The humour owed something to the Margaret Rutherford-Peter Sellers comedy *The Smallest Show on Earth* (1957), but scored chiefly through its portrait of industrial south Wales and a resilient community under duress. Bayly had placed his previous 1984 comedy, *Aderyn Papur* (And Pigs Might Fly), against a background of industrial recession, this time in the kind of north Wales quarry town hitherto sadly neglected in all Welsh drama. Bayly was virtually the first Welsh TV drama director since S4C's advent to make pertinent (and occasionally riveting) points about vital and current social and political developments in Wales within genre features of wide appeal.

The drift towards contemporary work was also obvious in film-makers who had built up a track record of 'period' drama. Paul Turner followed up his First World War epic *Hedd Wyn*, a complex and visually resourceful study of the loves and slightly ambivalent pacifism of the fated farmer-poet Ellis Evans with *Cwm Hyfryd* (Pleasant Valley) (1992). This downbeat drama, as relentless as *The Happy Alcoholic*, centred on an unemployed miner's increasing alienation from, and suspicions of, his wife and her relationship with a Patagonian seeking his Welsh roots. The film, while pivoting around the domestic drama, wove in fascinating issues of language and culture that had also driven *Boy Soldier*. Turner later made a modern thriller and revenge drama *Dial* (1994) which had moments of raw power but was marred by prurience and psychological implausibilities.

Caernarfon-based Alun Ffred Jones, of Ffilmiau'r Nant, best known for his versions of the gentle and parochial stories of Wil Sam Jones, declared in the 'nineties a willingness to handle more 'relevant' modern material. He produced *Cylch Gwaed* (In the Blood) (1992), directed by Tim Lyn, a persuasively downbeat tale of a boxer seeking vainly to fight his way out of penury and his stultifying milieu.

The Nant film won awards at the Celtic Film Festival, and spawned a follow up feature. In 1997 Alun Ffred directed a modern revenge drama *Tylluan Wen* (The White Owl) for S4C from a script by Angharad Jones, written before she replaced Dafydd Huw Williams as the channel's drama commissioner.[11]

The Jones drama with its distant echoes of the Blodeuwedd story, and *Branwen* (1994, dir. Ceri Sherlock, producer Angela Graham), dealing with a Welsh girl's disastrous involvement in Irish politics, showed the continuing inspiration of the Mabinogi mythology on dramatists able to draw modern analogies.

The appointment of Merioneth-born contemporary novelist Angharad Jones, 1995 Prose Medal winner at the National Eisteddfod, and still in her early thirties, seemed to indicate S4C's increasing awareness of a need to raise writing standards and to produce work homing in on modern life. No one underestimated her task, and Alun Ffred Jones was not alone in the mid-nineties in pointing to "a chronic lack of investment in screenwriting in both Welsh and English", claiming this militated against improved standards. But he also felt broadcasting executives in Wales had a "colonised mentality" – "so it's difficult to earn respect as writers and directors within the country, and London judgements are all too easily accepted."

The most successful of Welsh language drama directors Endaf Emlyn continues to give the lie to those who would decry Welsh talent. He moves easily from period pieces, including his masterpiece *Un Nos Ola Leuad* (One Full Moon) (1991) – arguably the finest film ever to have been made for television in Wales – to contemporary dramas, such as his 1997 S4C domestic comedy drama/road movie *Provence*. Emlyn's work has included genre features, and semi-autobiographical or youthful rites-of-passage material *Stormydd Awst* (Storms of August) (1988) or *Mapiwr* (The Making of Maps). His recent dramas reflect an increasing maturity in handling complex ideas and his growth in stature as a director has proved some vindication of S4C's policy of regular commissions to indigenous companies. Faced with no intimidating expectations, Emlyn, working with his own Cardiff based production company Gaucho, has developed at his own pace. He was able to experiment on *Stormydd Awst*, set in his native Pwllheli, and with frenetic and amusingly eclectic S4C dramas (*Gaucho* – a 'Welsh Western' (1984), *The Man Who Stole Christmas* (1985), and *Y Cloc* (The Clock) (1986) before moving on to the more substantial and mature works which sealed his reputation. *Un Nos Ola Leuad*, his film of redemption-through-suicide based on Caradog Prichard's novel, represented a quantum leap forward. It proved a flawlessly executed and heart-rendingly hermetic study of guilt, with Emlyn moving back and forth seamlessly in time. In *Gadael Lenin*, ostensibly a comedy set on a south Wales school trip to Leningrad/St Petersburg, Emlyn explored issues and notions of individual and creative loyalty, worth, and self-expression. In *Mapiwr*, his most cinematic movie – beautifully shot by Nina Kellgren and with narrative and stylistic echoes of the 1993 cinema movie *The Cement Garden* (directed by Wales-based Andrew Birkin) – Emlyn explored burgeoning sexuality in an over-heated family setting, upending audience expectations after setting us up for a more conventional mystery thriller.

Angharad Jones now feels it's high time S4C nailed its colours to the contemporary drama mast. Jones and script editor Dwynwen Berry are, significantly, both admirers of John Owen's work. His *Yn Gymysg Oll i Gyd*, S4C's 1996 St David's Day drama, dealt with schizophrenia – a hugely difficult subject – in an accessible way and with "maturity and sophistication," Jones feels.[12] Berry cites Owen's use of "colourful but correct idioms" and "authentic street talk". Much of this distinctive personal slant emerged in his comprehensive-school series *Pam Fi, Duw?*[13]

Angharad Jones wants to see modern drama dealing with the issues and preoccupations concerning today's population – but that, she says, "doesn't mean the dramas must be earnest. I'd like to stress the Importance of Not Being Earnest".[14]

Jones herself has written for the drama series *Coleg* and *Pengelli* and the soap *Dinas*. Her first single drama *Un Dwy Tair* (One, Two, Three) featuring three girls and set on a canal barge was refreshingly contemporary with much acerbic humour, setting the tone for her later work and preoccupations. It's perhaps not unlike *Tair Chwaer* (Three Sisters), Gaucho's contemporary amusingly earthy drama about the lifestyles of three girls in a band.

Jones feels that S4C drama writers would benefit from broadening their outlook. She feels she's gained much from the European-based SOURCES course and her script *Tylluan Wen* (The White Owl) derived from her Eisteddfod prize-winning novel *Y Dylluan Wen* but also, originally, from an English script she wrote under the SOURCES tutelage of sometime Ingmar Bergman collaborator Gunilla Jensen.[15]

Jones points out, justifiably, that the sincerity of a work counts much more than whether a drama is period or contemporary. Significantly she's most pleased with modern work delving into ordinary lives with humour and compassion. She takes pride in the first two first series of *Tair Chwaer* (directed, respectively by Endaf Emlyn and Cardiff's Emlyn Williams) and particularly the writing of Siwan Jones which has garnered her two successive BAFTA Cymru awards, not to mention Best Actress awards in successive years for Donna Edwards and Sharon Morgan. She's an admirer of Mei Jones, writer of *C'Mon Midffild* (C'Mon Midfield), and the humour of Paul Turner's 1998 *Porc Pei* (chiefly for its skillful construction and script by Wynford Ellis Owen).[16]

Yet, as she says, the channel cannot afford to discount fine work set in the past or to discard the contributions of mavericks such as Siôn Humphreys who has directed more than twenty single dramas ranging from 'modern' drama to literary classics, without quite finding a consistently satisfying visual style. Humphreys, fascinated by nuances of language and character motivation, is capable of such outstanding work as *Teulu Helga* (Helga's Family) (1985) and *Yr Alltud* (The Exile) (1989) and often employs highly theatrical devices.

Angharad Jones sets great store on established and dependable writers who can be relied on to deliver contemporary scripts – such as Meic Povey – *Nel* (1990) and *Sul Y Blodau*, (1988), for instance, but also feels the channel hasn't focused sufficiently on the feminine perspective in drama. We might reasonably expect this perceived dearth to be remedied by more contributions from an S4C distaff 'stable' – Siwan Jones, Manon Rhys, Eigra Lewis Roberts and Delyth Jones.[17]

S4C, since 1995, has been committed to providing one or two dramas each year for theatrical pre-transmission release (with a 35mm print) and spends £1.5m on these potential cinema movies, culled from a total £11 million drama budget (compared with Channel Four's 1995 £12 million on feature length drama alone).[18]

It's imperative that more of the domestic television drama continues to appeal, predominantly to the teens, twentysomethings and thirtysomethings. Angharad Jones would like to win over much of the Welsh language heartland audience in mid, north and west Wales (and traditionally conservative and middle aged). The nature of the viewers has undoubtedly weighed heavily on S4C executives loth to experiment despite numerous criticisms that much of the channel's material is pussyfooting and staid. It's hard, for example, to think of another Welsh Fourth Channel work as controversial or sexually explicit as its 1994 drama *Dafydd*, (dir. Ceri Sherlock), centred on a Welsh rent boy in Amsterdam, or *Atgof*, the same director's superbly controlled, impressionistic poetic fragment based on a homosexual – and literary – love affair.

Former S4C programme controller Deryk Williams always stressed that ratings would be crucial as long as the channel had such a narrow audience spectrum. The audience ratings success of the uninspired 1995 St David's Day film *Tom Nefyn*, a disappointingly conventional biopic from Cardiff's Scan company about the religious 'heretic' of the 'twenties, led one former programme controller Euryn Ogwen Williams, (later in charge of digital operations for the channel) to worry that it could drive the hierarchy deeper into the trenches and inspire more conservative programming.[19] Certainly at least one recent period venture designed to appeal to rural audiences proved a critical failure. The 1996 American co-production *Y Fargen* (The Proposition) (made in English and Welsh versions with separate leads, Theresa Russell and Patrick Bergin for the US audience; Aneurin Hughes and Gillian Elisa for domestic consumption), was an insipid affair, with a woebegone script centred around a cattle drive in the aftermath of the Napoleonic Wars, and indifferent female performances. Despite occasional ventures into more problematic political territory, for example with *Boy Soldier,* Gareth Wynn Jones's underrated terrorist drama *Ysglyfaeth* (Prey) (1984) and the Ceri Sherlock/Angela Graham feature *Branwen* (1994), Sianel Pedwar Cymru has opted for caution too much in the past in deference to its core audience. The prevailing conservative ethos at Llanishen immediately before Angharad Jones's arrival undoubtedly created tensions, reflected in director Tim Lyn's decision to kick over the traces. He reworked the latter episodes of the second series of *Pris Y Farchnad* (The Market Price) (1995) – centred around west Wales auctioneers – into lively, violent and raunchy action melodrama – a world removed from the source material of the first series. "I wanted to look into the dark side of those characters," says Lyn, an outspoken critic of S4C who feels there is an alarming paucity of good writing and actors working through the Welsh language and that many dramas fail to fulfil audience expectations. "With *Pris Y Farchnad* I wanted to use the language in a more realistic context, the kind of context viewers of genre films recognise, and to acknowledge some of the dark dealings which go on in any community, and which S4C don't tend to wish to reflect in their modern dramas. There's a reverence for language in Wales that is too stultifying, the language in a sense is old fashioned, it lacks modern idioms. It's even hard to swear in Welsh, and even harder to justify to the S4C authority characters swearing."[20]

Lyn found the Wil Roberts' script pedantic and staid, and the characters stereotypical. He reworked the scripts with his actors to explore much more graphically the modern world, dealing with fallible characters and volatile relationships, and creating visceral and idiosyncratic setpieces which prompted the press to make fanciful *Twin Peaks* comparisons.... The response indicated that S4C's potential audience might be less conservative than the channel's decision-makers appear to think – with the series peaking at 145,000 viewers – a record for any drama series on the channel (and far above the 90,000 viewers netted by *Tom Nefyn*). S4C then allowed Lyn freedom in contracting writers in a unique experiment for the third series of *Pris Y Farchnad*. The director formalised closer relationships with the performers – with actors such as Catherine Tregenna, Eluned Jones and Wyn Bowen Harries all receiving script credits. Lead characters were reduced from fifteen to four, with emphasis placed on dramatically intense, often squally marital and extra-marital relationships, in a drama laced with gallows humour. Lyn claims S4C disliked the third series, switched it from a projected winter peak-time to a less accessible slot. The audience plummeted to 45,000 and Lyn has since received no more S4C work – strange from a drama department supposedly committed to more modern ideas.

To writer John Owen, a pedantic Welsh language puritanism in contemporary drama is anathema and can militate against good writing. Owen feels bilingualism is a natural vehicle for dramatists in much of Wales. "My father doesn't speak Welsh and *Pam Fi, Duw?* (Why Me, God?) is bilingual for instance. I use Welsh idioms translated into English, non-Welsh speakers from my community don't feel threatened by that." What's needed, Owen feels, is "more confidence in intrinsically Welsh material whether in the English or Welsh language, and writers prepared to write about contemporary life and what they experience and know."[21]

The digital era may lead to more opportunities (though it might produce cheaper programming and fiercer competition) but increasingly in S4C – and in the English language, for that matter – the emphasis must be on producing work of innate value and pertinence to Wales. This drama, while offering insights into – and a mirror to – Welsh life with all its facets, should ideally be capable of transcending national boundaries to garner festival screenings and overseas sales. Welsh film-makers and drama producers, working through English or Welsh, must be confident enough to seek co-production deals between channels and with other nations for multilingual films (appropriately subtitled) as opposed to the kind of back-to-back Welsh/English productions with Channel Four which characterised the '80s (e.g. *Owain Glyndwr* and Stephen Bayly's *The Works* (1988)).

The broadcasters, with various short-term initiatives in the late 'nineties, have been slightly more willing to accept experiments in form and content in the interest of broadening audience horizons, but more generous funding from London or ITV centralised coffers is needed to give young directing and acting talent in Wales the opportunity to do consistently good work. Increasingly, one suspects, the brighter talents will drift away from the Welsh broadcasters (and perhaps even the country) as they seek funding further afield, through Europe or the Lottery. You can't help sensing an increasing impatience at the dearth of opportunities for film course graduates, for example, at the university colleges in Newport, Caerleon, Cardiff and the University of Glamorgan at Pontypridd. Given the history of the last two decades – with BBC Wales under-funded (and under-valued in London), S4C cutting programme costs and the ITV sector chasing lowest common denominator audiences, it is small wonder many promising Welsh film-makers and producers despair of finding fulfilment within the television drama of their own nation.

Notes

1. Karl Francis interviewed by the author, and memo to Michael Jackson, January 1997. A Dylan/Caitlin project directed by Chris Monger was due to start filming from another script, and under another title, in June 2000.
2. The present writer was involved in this project through most of 1996.
3. Dave Berry, 'Film and Television in Wales', in John Hill and Martin McLoone (eds.), *Big Picture, Small Screen* (Academic Research Monograph 16/ John Libby Media/ University of Luton Press, 1995). Phil John went on to direct the superb sex comedy *Suckerfish* (1999), as part of a BBC/Sgrîn short films initiative.
4. Dave Berry, *Wales and Cinema, The First 100 Years* (University of Wales Press: Cardiff, 1994).
5. Interview with Gwilym Owen, *Madam Wen*'s producer and the then director of Bwrdd Ffilmiau Cymraeg, May 13, 1991.
6. See 'Film and Television in Wales' in *Big Picture, Small Screen*, as above.
7. Interviews with Paul Turner in June 1995, Alan Clayton, Aug 14, 1997 and Meic Povey, Aug 31, 1997. Michael Balcon, *A Lifetime of Films* cited in Jeffrey Richards, *Films and British National Identity* (Manchester University Press: Manchester, 1997).
8. Clayton, *ibid.*
9. Geraint Morris (1941-1997) was best known for his BBC work, notably as producer-director of *The Onedin Line* and producer of *Casualty* and *Juliet*

Bravo, but he was senior drama consultant to HTV from 1994, producing the detective series. Menna Richards, HTV broadcasting director, claimed Morris "revitalised HTV's drama department."

10. See Bayly's article, 'Sianel Pedwar Cymru – the Welsh Perspective' in *Sight and Sound,* 1983.
11. Interview, Angharad Jones, Aug 6, 1997.
12. Interview, Angharad Jones, as above.
13. Interview, Angharad Jones, as above.
14. As Jones acknowledged in the interview above.
15. Interview, above. Alun Fred Jones, director of *Tylluan Wen* (interviewed, as above), has also stressed the value of SOURCES.
16. Angharad Jones, interview Mar 2, 1999.
17. Angharad Jones, interview, Aug 20, 1997 and Mar 2, 1999.
18. 'Film and Television in Wales' in John Hill and Martin McLoone eds., *Big Picture, Small Screen,* as above. The S4C theatrical release commitment has, alas, proved merely theoretical.
19. Interview with Euryn Ogwen Williams, Aug 4, 1997.
20. Interview with Tim Lyn, Aug 20, 1997.
21. Interview with John Owen, Aug 15, 1997.

This Town Ain't Big Enough
for the Both of Us
Darryl Perrins

Twin Town, released by Polydor in April 1997 at a cost of just 1.7 million, is at the time of writing the most commercially successful film to deal with Wales since *How Green Was My Valley* (1941). Here however, it would seem the comparisons end. *How Green Was My Valley* being a sentimental Hollywood melodrama, drawing upon fanciful Celtic imagery akin to Scottish tartanry and kailyard to create, as Peter Stead put it, a "mythical Shangri-La."[1] *Twin Town* appears to be at odds with all this. Kevin Allen's first feature, a black comedy, introducing us to the world of the twins Jeremy and Julian [played by real life brothers Rhys and Llyr Ifans], a pair of jobless delinquents who cut a drug-induced swathe, via a variety of stolen cars, across the "denuded reality of urban Swansea".[2] Here the grannies of *How Green Was My Valley* have tossed their tall hats asunder, to swap prescribed medicines for magic mushrooms to gain "good relief." The male voice underclass has replaced the massed male working class and is reduced to going on the 'hobble' and singing karaoke for its supper. Meanwhile, 'mam's' tidy and expansive terrace in the hills has been superseded by the cramped confines of a caravan, squeezed between the entry and exit wound of the M4 corridor and the now doomed Baglan Bay chemical works. The traditional family so central in *How Green* has now become dysfunctional, and big sister no longer hankers for the love of a preacher man, for she's too busy working as a receptionist in a massage parlour by day and doing tricks for bent bobbies by night. On the other side of the divide the coal masters, scab labour in tow, have been displaced by villainous businessmen and cocaine-dealing undercover cops at the top of the food chain in the pre-millennium undergrowth.

A somewhat jarring popular vision of Wales one could argue, seeing as it was released in the month of the Labour landslide, in a year when the voters of Wales gave the new Assembly its mandate, and at a time when the Asian Tiger economies were still taking the bait and prowling ever westward. Spearheading this revival were Welsh bands like Catatonia, Super Furry Animals and The Manic Street Preachers, who were climbing the national charts and devolving cultural power away from the centralising onus of 'Cool Britania', and into the provincial domain of what the press were calling 'Cool Cymru.'

Just how 'cool' this Cymru was, however, was never questioned as the Welsh establishment, 'part' of our cosy liberal 'consenting' proto-nation, hijacked the medium and in some cases the message of these so-called 'indie' bands. A prime example of this process is the media's incorporation of Catatonia's *International Velvet* – a song which has a single verse (sung in Welsh), extracts of which translate as: *"wake up sleepy Wales, land of song; the weakness is deep, the flame is small... I found the true paradise of Rhyl,"* lyrics which appear to set up the choris (sung in English): *"Every day, when I wake up, I thank the Lord I'm Welsh"* as ironic. The BBC soon picked up on this chorus as a patriotic talisman, detaching it from its ambiguous surroundings, thus turning any conceivable descent into consent, to accompany a variety of trailers to promote national sporting events. The currency of this partitioned chorus quickly gained favour, and reached its zenith when it was used almost as an alternative national anthem, or rather more fittingly in this land of 'New Labour' – national sound-bite, at the climax of the *Voices of a Nation* concert in Cardiff Bay, to mark the official opening of the Assembly in May of 1999. Watching the television coverage of the chorus being repeated *ad nauseam* by old war horses like Tom Jones, Shirley Bassey and Bonnie Tyler, to an audience graced by the presence of Queen Elizabeth II, it struck me just what this new Welsh 'hip' was made of, it is, I am sad to say, made of plastic.

This was the cumulation perhaps, of a method of assimilation that had begun during the build-up to the referendum vote in September 1997, when the 'Yes' campaign had targeted the stars of 'Cool Cymru' by sending out slogan-bearing t-shirts to recording studios. On the night of the event they were employed back-stage in various darkened bars and clubs to lend their voice to the call, and epitomise New Labour's buzzword for the day 'Inclusivity.' However, old habits die hard and at the legitimate 'high-key' end of proceedings out front at the national count centre in Cardiff, during the intervals between results, huge video screens were pumping out tourist board images of Wales: Anthony Hopkins' Snowdonia (now literally), Bardic boathouses etc... to the sound track of a male voice choir. Try as I might, I could not hear the nihilism of Nicky Wire lyrics over the rich baritone, nor see the sprawling red brick of my own council estate *mamwlad* (homeland) in this patriotic collage of 'inclusivity.' Judging by the narow majority for the Assembly (0.6% from a turnout that just scraped 50%), many other would-be voters also had problems recognising their Wales in this "Shangri-La" of democracy.

The dragon has it appears, not only two tongues, but two faces with which to hang them from, and it is this rich vein of emotional contradiction, institutional and cultural deceit that *Twin Town's* comedy aims to uncover and make sense of. "Ambition is critical," ironically exclaims Terry, the bent and psychotic Scottish copper played by Dougray Scott, near the beginning of the film, reading out loud the reconstituted Dylan Thomas 'quote' now cast in stone in the pavement outside Swansea railway station. He is quickly advised about its correct origin by his more educated and cautiously crooked colleague, the Welshman Greyo, played by Dorian Thomas. "It's a play on words. He said Swansea is the graveyard of ambition and he was right, the council came up with that." This disclosure combined with the next scene which has Terry and Greyo closing a cocaine deal with a Cockney courier, in the re-built version of Thomas's regular coffee shop 'The Kardomah', at once distances the film from the triumphalism of the hour, and the heritage image of Thomas so meticulously nurtured by Swansea City Council. Thus reminding us that the author of such definitive Welsh works as *Under Milk Wood* and *Fern Hill,* was indeed himself an addict, not adverse to bouts of irreverence. It is with this disparaging flipside of Welsh imagery that the film quickly links itself, retitling Swansea "a pretty shitty city", and in doing so mirroring the sentiments of the Bard himself, who came from this "blousey town,... a dingy hell." On the edge of "this arsehole of the Universe, this hymnal blob, this pretty sick, fond sad Wales". The "land of my fathers, my fathers can keep it".[3]

Needless to say, this disrespect in the face of a growing cult of optimism and 'National confidence', led the film to be criticized from liberal as well as traditionally conservative quarters. Ben Thompson in *Sight and Sound* taking the patronizing view that such disrespect could not come from within Wales, rather that "the persuasive pall of cynicism which seems to hang over the project is pure Groucho Club". This ignores the fact that Swansea is Kevin Allen's home town, indeed, most of his family appear in the film, and that co-screen writer and Swansea-Jack-of-all-trades Paul Durden is far more likely to be found in the rehearsal rooms called "Purgatory" he owns and runs for local bands, than bantering with the media elite over continental lagers at The Groucho Club. Thompson went on to attack it from a moral standpoint, remarking that it had "a streak of sadism as wide as the M4 running through it"[4], while, as Nigel Morris noted in *Planet*, "The film was attacked by clergy, whose warnings of copycat poodle beheadings surpassed the satire on screen – perpetuating a century of mistrust epitomised by the poem 'Beware of the Cinema' by Reverend Thomas David Evans."[4]

In many respects, these responses recall the reaction to the publication of Caradoc Evans's *My People* in 1915, a collection of short stories depicting a feuding and spiteful Cardiganshire peasantry held in strict hierarchy by an oppressive religion. The book came out a time when much of Wales was still feeling the ripples of the last great revival of 1904-5, and the pulpits were being used as recruiting stations for the front. The wider popular image was still that of the "land of the white gloves".[6] A harmonious peasant utopia embedded within the popular imagination via the transition of the mountainscapes and ruins of Richard Wilson and Turner, available on affordable prints and tablemats, and novels like *The Wooing of Myfannwy* by Allen Raine. Evans' vision ran counter to these establishment images, therefore he faced the wrath of its mouthpiece in Wales, *The*

Western Mail, whose reviewer labelled it "a squalid repellent picture", while its letters page over the ensuing weeks was to brand it "a farrago of filth" and "the literature of the sewer"[7], reactions that surely must have prompted its attempted ban in Cardiff. In contrast the popular press in England applauded it, allowing it to become a best seller in its genre, going through three reprints in as many months.

The point to all this is that in the case of *My People* and *Twin Town* and their public reception, we see satire revealed as the 'comedy of errors,' undercutting the zeitgeist. Their popularity a barometer of conscious dissent against the establishment's continuing grand narrative of pretension, thus allowing feelings to surface that are commonly held but rarely spoken, because they may be deemed disrespectful, fatalistic, unsavoury or even unpatriotic. In this respect, like its irreverent predecessor *My People, Twin Town* is a kick-back, to productively misappropriate the words of Gwyn Alf Williams, against those that have the real power to construct the "artifact" of Wales: "to make and remake Wales, day after day, year by year".[8]

Of course in a wider sense, to borrow from the work of Neale and Krutnik: "From Aristotle on, and in contrast to tragedy, comedy was for centuries the most appropriate genre for representing the lives not of the ruling classes, of those with extensive power, but of the 'middle' and 'lower' orders of society, whose power was limited and local, and whose manners, behaviour and values were considered by their betters to be either trivial or vulgar."[9] The case of *Twin Town* would appear to fit within this tradition by distancing itself from satire *per se*; a 'tasteful,' subtle and often exclusive tradition inhabited by the likes of Wilde and the Ealing comedies, through mobilizing more traditional popularist and 'tasteless' forms of comedy, to mock bourgeoisie attitudes and by painting its satire in broad iconoclastic strokes across a comic book canvas.

Indeed at times, when watching the film, one could almost believe one was sitting through a high octane climactic Welsh 'Carry-On.' Witness, for example, its use of a barely developed ensemble cast heavy with stereotype. The most extreme case being Keith Allen's x-rated pantomime farmer: the sheep-shagging Emrya (clearly a pun on enema). A slap-stick physicality which delivers comic beatings and accidents, and a cinema language which through a comic book and home-spun non-realism, owes more to Carry On director Gerald Thomas than the painterly European furrow now ploughed in Wales by Welsh directors like Marc Evans.

An approach it also shares with the Carry On series is illustrated in its farcical and highly disposable plot, itself encompassed within a single dream-like structure, which creates in its "them and us" dichotomy a privileged audience (one that is aware of the joke), and one made up of voyeurs. We are made aware of this as the opening credits roll, via a point of view slow motion tracking shot which forces the viewers gaze into a bourgeoisie metropolitan 'daydream' of de-industrialised urban provincial life. As the camera slowly tracks into the high summer of a modest Swansea suburb at charabanc level, "we" become cultural tourists and, as such, are addressed by its inhabitants. An old man in a white vest waves at us smiling a toothless grin; a hopelessly unfashionable middle-aged guy, long haired, moustached, in gaudy shorts and Hawaiian shirt crosses the pavement in front of an off licence, and raises his can of strong lager in our direction in a 'Cheers' motion. Two nurses uncover our peep show desires and assumptions of open sexuality by raising the skirts of their uniforms provocatively; and finally a biker takes time out from fixing his Kawasaki by the roadside to remind us of the dangerous thrill we receive from travelling through the working class jungle, by fixing us with a glare and issuing the 'V' sign from his greasy and sovereign-ringed fingers. All this is played out to the M.O.R. sounds of Petula Clark singing 'The Other Man's Grass is Always Greener.' The last line before we cut into the plot, lingering and setting the distance from which the film must be viewed: "Be thankful for what you've got."

The Plot: after establishing this perspective, the film returns us to the conventional exchange of looks between characters and we are introduced to the two main narrative lines. The first of these revolves around two under-cover cops: the psychotic Scot Terry and the more cautious Greyo, the businessman Cartwright and their increasing involvement in cocaine dealing. The second centring on the twins, Jeremy and Julian Lewis, and their delinquent lifestyle of drug-taking and joy riding, which is interrupted by an increasingly dark spiral of revenge. The source of this interruption is Cartwright's refusal to pay their father Fatty compensation for an injury while he was doing a 'hobble' on Cartwright's rugby club-house roof. The twins' first action of revenge has them urinating over Cartwright's teenage daughter Bonnie during her karaoke set at 'Baron's Nightclub', in a scene that appears to be a 'golden shower' reworking of the pig's blood humiliation at the high-school prom in *Carrie*. For this they receive a sound beating on the Mumbles Mile, which they counter à la *Godfather*, by leaving Cartwright's wife's poodle's severed head in the marital bed. In reply to this Cartwright orders the death of the Lewis's family dog, Cantona. This is botched by Terry, who in an attempt to burn the dog alive, ignites the Calor gas bottle next to the Lewis's caravan, killing the twins' father Fatty, mother Jean and sister Aidie. This act alerts the until now, 'in the dark' Greyo, to Cartwright's involvement in the deaths. He then faces Cartwright down and offers him a man-slaughter charge. Cartwright responds by informing him that he has a stash of cocaine with Greyo and Terry's prints all over them, which he will use if charged. Terry and the increasingly conscious-ridden Greyo then fit-up Dai Rees, the local 'karaoke king', with the crime. Dai's alibi that he was with Cartwright's daughter Bonnie on the night of the explosion, sends Cartwright into a jealous and violent rage, at the family's luxury home The Ponderosa, in the Mumbles, and he forces Bonnie to make a statement denying Dai's claim. Meanwhile, the twins have stolen the hearse with their father's body still in it from outside the church where their family were due to be buried, and taken it to a secret location. Back at The Ponderosa, Cartwright's shaken wife Lucy, receives a phone call from Greyo. They meet secretly and Lucy reveals to Greyo the location of the incriminating cocaine bags; in the life jacket in Cartwright's speedboat. The twins then arrive at The Ponderosa seeking revenge, and truss Cartwright up in a noose connected to his automatic garage door. Before doing this, Cartwright blurts out that Terry was responsible for the deaths. Upon leaving Cartwright, they take his car and speedboat, unaware of its contents, from the garage, before attacking Terry in his home.

The film then cuts to Mumbles pier where a massed male-voice choir is preparing to lament their deceased member Fatty, to the deep, while out in Swansea bay the twins prepare to lower Fatty's coffin with Terry strapped to it, overboard. Back on land, Greyo and Lucy arrive at The Ponderosa to collect the cocaine, and Lucy inadvertently strangles her husband by attempting to open the garage door. Back out to sea, the twins set their father's final wish "to be buried at sea with a big choir and a Welsh flag" into motion, by firing a flare up into the night sky. Greyo and Lucy see the flare and rush down to the pier, slowly putting the pieces together as the gruesome denouement unfolds. With the coffin, Terry and a quickly following Welsh flag lost to Swansea bay, the twins turn the boat around and head for Morocco. The plot now closed, we are returned to the audience point of view of the opening credits via an aerial shot that rises and carries our gaze up from the water and along the pier, before we pull back and bank away ever higher into the night sky. The pier fades to black behind us as 'we' are lulled back into the safety of a more acceptable Welsh daydream by the soft tones of the choir's rendition of *Myfanwy*.

The strength of this narrative, complete with its genre staple of a 'happy ending,' lies in the ease with which the audience can suspend belief, just as one does with the improbable and often random structure of the Carry On narratives. Once this disbelief is established, the highly animated social and cultural satire within this dream of reality, particularly to its 'privileged' audience, is allowed to enter fully into the foreground. In the Carry On series, the comedy was largely aimed at notions of British 'restraint' and 'respectability,' and its head-to-head cross-class collision within the context of communal institutions like the hospital or the campsite. Here, the animal nature of the human being was championed, largely with reference to Sid James' preference for idleness over hard work, and sex over abstinence. Moving away from the drug dealing/cycle of revenge narrative, the social and cultural satire of *Twin Town* also comes from rebellion against an "institution"; the "institution" in question being Wales. Sid James's chirpy cockney being replaced as the nucleus of rebellion by the nihilism of the Lewis brothers, who refuse to engage with the sentimental and anachronistic universe that rails all around them, within which other characters struggle to hang on to notions of 'Welshness.' Indeed it is this credo of indifference that marks them out as true anti-heroes, in the passionate Celtic cultural milieu. Even the critically acclaimed vision of Wales that *House of America* (1997) provided has, at its heart, the figure of 'Sid', the doomed romantic. The twins on the other hand are purely visceral creations, whose actions are opportunistic, akin to Sid James' animal functions. It is this quality more than anything else that allows them to put the anachronisms of Wales into focus.

These anachronisms soon become clear, and are highlighted by director/screenwriter Kevin Allen and co-screenwriter Paul Durden's knowledge and use of Welsh cultural iconography. Early on in the film this is put to good use to indicate where the film's loyalties lie, when the twins share a bath in the family caravan. This evokes memories of the communal tin bath scenes that feature so heavily in traditional, cinematic and literary representations of South Walian industrial life. However, the bath they take is not in order to cleanse away the filth of the pit, but rather to wash away the sweat of exhilaration after a 'nightshift' of joy-riding and criminal activity. Thus, this signifier of traditional Welsh family life and the Protestant work-ethic behind it, is turned on its head. Further, it becomes the site of dialogue between the two brothers that begins to set them apart from the other characters, as they discuss that anathema to South Walian sporting mores: soccer. Julian questions Jeremy in Tarantino-esque pop-culture trivia obsessive style, as to why Cardiff City have triangular corner flags, while Swansea City have squares, the forfeit for a wrong answer being a long 'toke' of marijuana on a shower hose-come-"bong."

Compare this, if you will, with the later 'field of dreams' turning to nostalgia in crisis of Ben Cartwright, played by William Thomas. Cartwright, when faced with Greyo's manslaughter charge at the rugby club wake for the Lewis family, dispels Lucy and Greyo's anger when he evokes the *hwyl* inspired by the sublime talents of Phil Bennett and co, who turned the game around against Scotland at Murryfield in 1977. Greyo and Lucy are affected so much by this moving evocation that they relive the match with Cartwright who, having won them over exclaims, as he pulls out a hidden bag of cocaine from said rugby ball, covered in the fingerprints of both Terry and Greyo: "One minute we're in the shit, the next we get a result". Thus implying that if he is charged he will reveal Greyo's involvement in the cocaine deal. Far from being, as *Sight and Sound's* Ben Thompson suggests, an example of "Celtic sporting triumph as metaphor for national pride",[10] a reworking of the euphoric viewing of the video recording of Archie Gemmill's goal against Holland in 1978 by Renton in *Trainspotting* (1996); in this 'comedy of errors' it is a corrupt eulogy to the past, a warning of the irrationality and manipulative power of national sentiment, pronounced by the doomed Cartwright – a villain soon to be dispatched. Importantly, the scene also strikes at the very heart of Welsh national iconography, for as Cartwright triumphantly holds up the rugby ball and pulls out the 'stash', one can't help but compare the imagery with the opening scenes of *Easy Rider* (1969), and Peter Fonda's character Wyatt/ Captain America pushing his rubber hose full of dollar bills earned from a cocaine deal into the fuel tank of his chopper. The camera signifies the portent of this act by pulling back and lingering to reveal the stars and bars across the fuel tank's body work. The rugby ball and its contents serve a similar cultural purpose – there's something rotten in the State of 'Aberflyarf.'

In comparison, the twins' use of drugs (importantly, they never use the more exclusive drug cocaine dealt by the villains), to gain escape and oblivion, and their petty dealing with pensioners, from whom they buy prescribed 'downers' from, appears sincere and even benevolent. Meanwhile, the quasi-religious importance afforded to sport by Cartwright, Lucy and Greyo, is reduced by the twins to the level of *Trivial Pursuit* in the on-going sibling banter that they exchange, or mocked, as when they steal their parole officer's golf clubs and ape the middle class on the fairway. For the twins, the sacred signifier of Welshness that is Rugby Union, it's continuing patronage in Welsh cultural life, a fine example of the power of nostalgia, holds no significance at all. Indeed, as the twins perform hand-break turns in a stolen Cobra sports car across Cartwright's beloved rugby pitch, they are not even aware of their actions. To them it is just another arena within which to squeal the radials of indifference.

This twins' indifference also extends to language, in an environment where bilingualism has passed on to an educated middle class together with a rump of the older working class population. This position is succintly captured through the only Welsh dialogue scene, whcich is held between the educated cop Greyo and the drug-pushing pensioners Mr and Mrs Mort. For the twins' peers however, language is still a resonant source of identity, and known phrases and terms colour conversations, as illustrated by the twins' sister Aidie, who responds to her brothers' taunts that she is a prostitute with *"Ydw a nac ydw"*("I am and I'm not"). This 'wenglish' is further elaborated upon in the south by the employment of an array of 'words' that only appear to be Welsh. A good example of 'Wenglish' from *Twin Town* is *cwtch*, used by Chip, Dai Rees's karaoke DJ sidekick, when he suggests the Lewis family all 'cwtch up' in a triple decker single grave, rather than take up three sites. The twins sever this link by not entering into the sentimental linguistic privileging of 'Wenglish' and poor old Mrs Lewis, the twins' mother, is reduced in her working class milieu, to resorting to speaking Welsh to the family dog Cantona. To which her daughter Aidie responds: "Why do you speak to him in Welsh mam? You got him in Bristol, he can't understand a fucking word". Perhaps the suggestion here is that an ulpan beginners Cymraeg course in obedience for English canine incomers, may be the only future for the language in Wales!

Wales is still a singing nation however, and the twins' father Fatty Lewis, played by Huw Ceredig still finds room in the cramped caravan for a chapel organ. Fatty's belief in singing as a yardstick to national identity, is measured by his final wish, which is to be buried at sea under a Welsh flag, to the strains of a 'big choir.' However, this grand finale is not meant to extol an heroic past, as *Brassed Off* (1996) does, with its upbeat and dignified image of a brass band in a declining Northern town, replenished by youthful (and female) members, who overcome the odds to win the national competition at the Albert Hall. Rather, *Twin Town* presents the male-voice choir, whose roots lie in the Puritan impulse of the Chapels and their belief in the impropriety of anything but doxology, thus putting pay to Wales developing a popular and radical industrial folk tradition, as ageing and out of time, a once central institution long stripped of religious duties and now also the inter-generational framework offered by large scale single industry. Out on a limb, the choir in *Twin Town* falls back on what it does best: masquerade and the interpretation of popular standards. The ensemble take time out from preparing to lament Fatty to the deep, to rehearse their future without him, swapping what Kim Howells once called "penguin suits, aping the bourgeoisie"[11] for the casual clothes of light entertainment, and the high drama of the hymn for the 'choo choo' locomotive harmonies of Mungo Jerry's 'In the Summertime.' Within this reading, karaoke appears in the film, not as Fatty Lewis protests to Dai Rees: "What's killing Welsh choir music", but as its natural heir. Dai Rees becoming, in the land where continuity and change fuse, the 'karaochoirmeister' of the new millennium. From this position he rallies the massed youth of Swansea in Baron's Nightclub to join him in singing Petula Clark's 'Down Town,' and by default reminds us of the new democracy within Welsh singing practice (now you don't have to be 'good' at it, or male, to take part), and taunts Fatty Lewis while they both work on Cartwright's roof, with what can be seen as a mocking farewell tribute to the ageing male voice, with his rendition of Stephens and Greenaway's 'It's Gonna Be a Cold, Cold Christmas Without You.'

Perhaps it's important to stress at this juncture, that the reins of condoned satire are clearly held within the grip of the actions and comments of Welsh characters. This is a deeply embedded comic 'moral' which the outsider, Scottish undercover cop Terry transgresses at his peril. His disgust at all things 'Welsh' demonstrated throughout the film by an array of offences that range from the slighting of the national rugby team, to the stomach punch he delivers to one of the young 'Welsh bastards' in the children's kazoo band, is represented not as comedy, but as malevolent bigotry; a symptom of his increasingly criminal psychosis. The line therefore between the constructive criticism of healthy self-reflection and intolerance, is clearly drawn. In this respect, *Twin Town's* zealously guarded self-loathing acts as a rude 'Borsch Belt'[12] like awakening, to the comic realities of Welsh culture. A fitting counter-point to the comedy of the past embodied by the gushing sentimentality and 'Welsh' idiosyncrasy mimicked by the likes of Max Boyce and most recently the BBC Wales sitcom *Satellite City*. Perhaps then we have grown in confidence enough to stop laughing, as we did according to Kim Howells in 1980 "at an externally manufactured image of *our*selves [my italics] and one moreover which emphasises those characteristics which are least offensive and troublesome to those who govern us – like newspaper proprietors and television controllers."[13] In short we may be beginning to learn, to paraphrase Caradoc Evans, not to hate ourselves, but to like each other well enough to criticise our own behaviour.

There is, however, a regrettable step back from this highly therapeutic disrespect in the choice of football shirt the character Terry is dressed in for the last quarter of the film. This choice may have been made with an eye on Celtic-American box-office sales; more likely however, it reflects the particular attachments of executive producers Danny Boyle and Andrew MacDonald. Even so, by clothing Terry in a 'true blue' Glasgow Rangers home-strip, the film's overall scheme of representational bravery, highlighted by having a Scottish rather than an English 'bad guy' is damaged. This removes the arch-villain's 'Scottishness' and places it within a loyalist/British framework. The traditional good Celt bad Anglo-Saxon connotations, *à la Braveheart*, of this seemingly trivial move, warns us of the problems of confusing specific Welsh themes with broader Celtic agendas. One could even argue that it harks back to the dark days of Hollywood-Wales, when director John Ford fought out the battle for Irish emancipation on the Welsh soil of Richard Llewellyn's *How Green Is My Valley*.

If we return to the prospect of change running parallel with continuity, we can see it again repeated in images of labour within the film, whereby the father Fatty Lewis is replaced by his daughter Aidie, as the only one in the family with a steady job. Aidie's position as a part-time receptionist at a massage parlour mirrors the changes in de-industrialised society, whereby the patriarch no longer collects a living wage from a unionised occupation, and is instead faced with the prospect of either accepting a low-paid, temporary non-unionised position, or, supplementing his only 'dependable' income – social security, with 'hobbles.' In the face of a system that appears to have reneged on a deal fought out over decades, the road to retrieval of self-respect must lie in the black economy.

This leaves the likes of Fatty Lewis as easy prey for upwardly mobile entrepreneurs, like Bryn Cartwright, the real profiteers of the age. Aidie however, without the weight of this occupational tradition behind her, takes her place in the growing service sector. An area of work still, to a large extent, beyond the acceptable blue collar aspirations of the majority of male members of a traditional working class culture, within which most gender relationships hold firm. This is illustrated in the film by the almost exclusively male clientele of the rugby club house, by the obsessively protective relationship of the nouveau-riche likely lad Cartwright to his wife and daughter, and by the continuing domestic role of 'mam' Mrs Lewis, in her much reduced kitchen. With the durability of this dichotomy established, we are released from the easy fix of the likes of ex-steel workers taking up the opportunity of the new and 'liberating' area of service industry employment, and we are gladly saved from the sight of Fatty in a P.V.C. leotard *à la The Full Monty*. More importantly however, so is he.

Within this social context, Aidie and her fellow massage workers' new-found independence is neutered, and made doubly ironic as their role as workers and providers is dependent on the men's continuing role as sexual predators. Indeed, in perhaps the strongest and darkest scene in *Twin Town*, the glamour of proletarian flesh, constructed by *The Full Monty*, is stripped bare to reveal the soulless, economic exchange underneath, as an overweight middle-age masseuse matter-of-factly runs through her repertoire while puffing on a cigarette. Her pot-bellied and wheezing client Ivor, played by Kevin Allen's uncle Royston John, finally settling for a "Tits and handshandy". The visual iconography is unsettling here, for as the masseuse leans over her client, arms outstretched, one is reminded of the still image of Rachel Thomas, taken from *The Blue Scar* (1948), bending over her husband scrubbing his back in a tin bath next to the fire. A recurring image of Welsh womanhood to be found on book covers and at exhibitions across the land. Continuity and change are implicit again when comparing these images, for the roles and positions are still intact, only the arena from domestic to business has changed.

Fatty's search for occupational self-respect is highlighted by his refusal to put his name to the shoddy workmanship he is forced into by Cartwright on the club house roof. Moments later, his fall from a dodgy ladder becomes the slap-stick catalyst for the narrative's dissent into anarchy. It is only a short step from the visual humour of Fatty's fall from grace to the social commentary that follows, as Fatty's status as an uninsured worker relying on the philanthropy of employers is laid bare, as the family gather round his hospital bed. With the removal of any legal claim to compensation, it is his sons who must represent him in the post-unionised world of labour relations, where notions of individual honour have returned to replace the right of arbitration which was once so sorely fought for. Cartwright, a product of Thatcherite economic brutality, is however, no Robert Owen, and his refusal to pay compensation is only compounded by his thrusting of two tenners into the boys' hands, so they can go and buy some "Sticky sticky, and fuck off back to Noddy land".

They refuse to be bought off however, and it is this refusal, a conscious act of commitment on the part of the twins, to the 'lived history' of family loyalty and labour relations, that tears them away from their cultural inertia and indifference. Not so much "Everything Must Go" as everything *that matters* must go on. This action in particular marks *Twin Town* out, not as Derek Malcolm's review described it: "A baleful picture of a crumbling, hopelessly divided society, slouching toward anarchy",[14] but as a film whose central characters represent and are applauded by a disenchanted youth, that is the highly visceral and popular counterweight to the "brilliant cerebral contribution to the struggle to define Welshness"[15] that is *House of America* (1997). The twins battling for dignity through cultural nakedness and a degree of moral reinstatement through a sense of "lived history," within the anachronistic and premeditatedly immoral universe they find themselves in. With all other mechanisms removed, they are forced to put their own anachronism, revenge, in place. The consequences and warnings of which, the film makes brutally clear. *"Every day when I wake up, I thank the Lord I'm Welsh."*

Notes

1. P. Stead,'Wales in the Movies' in T. Curtis ed., *Wales the Imagined Nation* (Seren: Bridgend, 1986) p.172.
2. Luke Harding, 'Judgement Dai', *The Guardian*, September 16th, 1997.
3. D. Thomas, from *Selected Letters*, ed. C.Fitzgibbon, (Dent: 1956), quoted in the chapter: 'A Picnic in the Orchard: Dylan Thomas's Wales', by James A. Davies, in *Wales the Imagined Nation*, p.48-49.
4. B. Thompson, *Sight and Sound*, Vol.7 No.4, April, 1997, p.54.
5. N. Morris, 'Projecting Wales', *Planet* 126, December-January 1998, p.27
6. M. Stephens, in *The Oxford Companion to the Literature of Wales*, p.239, explains the phrase "Land of the white gloves" as a name for Wales, popular in late Victorian times, deriving from the custom of presenting judges with white gloves when there are no cases for them to try. The description reflects an idealized view of the Welsh as a people of superior moral standards. It essentially equates morality with keeping the law.
7. J. Harris ed., *Caradoc Evans: My People* (Seren: Bridgend, 1987) p.38.
8. Gwyn Alf Williams, from *When Was Wales?* A BBC Wales annual radio lecture broadcast on Radio Wales and Radio Cymru, 12 November, 1979.
9. S. Neale, and F. Krutnik, *Popular Film and Television Comedy* (Routledge: London, 1990) p.11.
10. B. Thompson, *Sight and Sound*, p.54.
11. K. Howells, Interview in *Planet* 51, June 1985, p.9-10. (Cited in John Osmond, *The Divided Kingdom* (Constable: 1988) p.134.
12. "The Borsch Belt" is a term to describe the comedy circuit that developed around the Catskill mountain vacation centres which catered for Jewish families, largely from New York. From where a comedy of 'Self-hate' developed, which was to later influence the neurotic self-parody of Woody Allen and Mel Brooks.
13. K. Howells, 'Plastic Max', in *ARCADE – Wales Fortnightly*, No 2, November 1980. (Cited in John Osmond, *The Divided Kingdom* (Constable: 1988) p.134.
14. D. Malcom, 'How Grim is Valley', a review of *Twin Town*, *The Guardian*, April 11th, 1997.
15. N. Morris, 'Projecting Wales', *Planet* 126, December-January 1998, p.26.

Diary of Two Mad Housewives
Fizzy Oppe

10th August 1998. I am sitting in the garden reading whilst my seven year old daughter and my one year old son play. I say I am reading but I am really indulging in that activity which Truman Capote called "watching anxiety copulating with depression" which is the most common pastime of any freelance film producer/actor/writer who hasn't worked for a couple of weeks. I have recently produced a Welsh language short fiction film which offered a small part to my baby son, but making short fiction films is no career for a forty-something mother and it's time to retrain into a proper job. To allay my increasing anxiety I have just come to a definite decision – I am going to study for my maths GCSE in the coming September and then do the one year training that would lead to work as a primary school teacher. A good plan and a sensible plan. I go into the house to answer the ringing telephone.

> I've just had a call from someone called Fergus at the BBC in Bristol – they like *Dune*, well they really like *Dune* and they want us to go to a meeting on Friday to discuss it, I said "yes."

It is my writer/director friend Catrin Clarke who had submitted a short fiction script to the BBC for the *10x10* series with my name attached as producer.

Over the next week Catrin writes another draft of the script and I draw up a budget. I'm still breast feeding Bryn and he never sleeps for longer than two hours at a stretch but it's amazing what you can do in two hours if you have to. Catrin has three children and is a single parent but hers are all school age, which is not a great advantage since it is the middle of the summer holidays. On the Friday morning we meet up at Teliesyn, a Cardiff film and television production company who I work with who will produce the film if we get beyond the first meeting.

We find a yellow folder and paste a photo of the sand dunes at Merthyr Mawr on the front, where Catherine wants to shoot the film, and we then enclose the newly drawn up budget (£72,000), a revised script and some photographs of selected actors that we've photocopied from the actors directory: *Spotlight*. It all feels very Blue Peter, cutting and sticking.

We leave our five children with my partner and drive to Bristol. We discuss tactics for the hour it takes us to get to Bristol city centre. These days you can attend short courses on how to pitch to commissioning editors – once you've achieved that all-important milestone of actually getting the first meeting. But it's difficult to get away to attend courses when you are the single parent of three children or the mother of a not yet weaned baby. During my career I have sat on the other side of the table on numerous occasions, mainly as a member of a publicly funded panel allocating money for film projects and once as the producer of four short films for BBC Wales/Sgrîn (then the Wales Film Council). From this perspective you are looking for informed enthusiasm and also the sense of someone you could work with and trust – a track record, however fledgling the film-maker's career, and most importantly the ability of the person who's being interviewed to conjure up the film in words. As part of our preparation I have remembered that Helen Rowlands from Ty Ffilm (the publicly funded film workshop in Cardiff) has been planning a day event with Jeremy Howe, *10x10's* Executive Producer for the Wales International Film Festival which is to be held in Cardiff this year. She has six *10x10* films in the office and we watch them to get an idea of editorial policy, production values and budgets. One of the films; *Queens Park Story* is a love story which utilises a post production technique made famous by the feature film *Babe* in which animals talk very realistically in lip synch. I reckon it must have cost at least £80,000. *Crocodile Snap* is a domestic drama involving children and a mother on a rather desperate day out in Blackpool. This has similar production concerns to *Dune*. There is a witty low budget 'art' film about a woman at sea on her bed and a documentary about apples which is inventive and difficult to price.

Catrin is less worried about the budget and more worried about the vocabulary of directing. How is she going to describe how she wants the film to look? We rehearse several phrases and I keep reminding her that Fergus has said they really like the script.

The meeting goes well. The 10x10 team are interested in Catrin. As part of the application, Catrin has sent them *Horse City,* the last film that we made together – another short – about a young pregnant woman isolated on a Cardiff housing estate who relates to the wild horses that roam freely, as they do in St. Mellons where Catrin was briefly housed with her three children. Jeremy is clearly interested in the subject matter of Catrin's films. Like all of Catrin's work it is loosely based on personal experience. One sequence in *Horse City* necessitated filming the birth of a foal. We had to shoot the sequence in January when very few mares are ready to foal. We put an appeal out on the Roy Noble radio show and were contacted by a Welsh Cob stud farm in Blaenau. Catrin and Tony Yates, the camera man, lived in Tony's four wheel drive for four days waiting for the mare to go into labour. Catrin's three children stayed with me and I drove backwards and forwards with food and encouragement. Tony had another job to go to on the Monday morning so on Sunday afternoon he had to leave Catrin with the camera and instructions on how to use it whilst I chased all over Cardiff for an acceptable replacement cinematographer. I arrive at the farm at 10 p.m. with the replacement, but Tony has returned because the mare has gone into labour and after all the waiting he really wants to shoot the sequence. The replacement cameraman and I watch the birth on a close circuit camera installed in the stable. The stable is full of the steam that is coming off the mare and I can see Tony shooting for as little as twenty seconds before having to clear the lens. The foal is born in its cowl and struggles free like a bird hatching from a rubbery shell. Tony gets it all in twenty second snatches.

We end up relaying this and other stories to Jeremy Howe and his colleagues before discussing business. The BBC *10x10* unit only have as little as £20,000 for their fiction films, Jeremy Howe explains, they don't expect the producer and director to get paid, they want to see the whole budget spent on what ends up on screen.

Horse City cost about £62,000 and I was hoping for progression. *10x10* is a network slot whilst *Horse City* was made by BBC

Wales. How are we going to make the film for £20,000 when the budget I have prepared estimates costs at nearer £70,000?

We've got five children between us, I plead with Jeremy Howe. He looks sympathetic but only has a strand budget of £160,000 for ten films. What about the love story with the talking animals, *Queens Park Story*, I say hopefully trying to find a precedent for a high budget *10x10*. But it turns out that *Queens Park Story* was made by a commercials company that managed to hide the costs of the post-production; *10x10* only gave them £24,000.

We leave the meeting sounding confident that we can find the additional money to make the film. The Arts Council of Wales (ACW) Lottery Unit would have been the obvious choice, but even with a fast track application (under £10k) we'd be pushed for time as the film has to be delivered by the end of March 1999. We can't shoot in the winter because the film is set in the summer and early November, which we mentally fix for the first day of shooting, is as late as we can feasibly go. The story of *Dune* involves a single mother on a council estate who is being threatened with eviction if she does not improve the state of her garden. An over zealous new environmental officer is running a competition for the best garden on the estate. Donna's next-door neighbours have a beautiful garden and they side with the council in trying to make Donna conform. The last shot of the film is of the mother (Donna) and her four children lying in the sun having transformed their garden into a dune landscape. There is not enough time to make a funding application to the ACW and shoot the film before winter comes and 10x10 want the film delivered by Easter 1999.

On the way back to Cardiff I dampen Catrin's excitement by being the pragmatic producer. It will cost me at least £68.00 per week to have Bryn put in full time childcare and then there is what we do with the other children after school. We both know how time consuming it is making fiction films, even very short ones, and the strain it puts on partners and children when you're in active pre-production, shooting and editing. If you can't even bring home a wage at the end of it all it's just a self-indulgent hobby.

"Or a calling card for better things," Catrin reminds me. "This is a *10x10* – a network BBC production, shown in peak viewing time. It's not a tokenistic marginal scheme destined for the graveyard slot after midnight on regional television and they've never made one from Wales before."

"That's alright for writers and directors," I grumble, "but nobody remembers who the producer of a short film is and anyway I've produced network drama before – I've been around the block a few times and I think we should get paid. We're a good team and you're a distinctive and unusual voice in British television. How can they expect to get films from working class communities that describe the experience of marginalised voices like single parents if they won't bloody well pay for them. You're the last person I know who should be making network dramas for no salary – you've got three children to support."

Fired with this argument I decide to take the script up to the BBC Wales Drama department on Monday morning to see if they could help find us some money for the film. Catrin has recently been on a writers lab organised by the newly appointed Head of Drama, Pedr James and his business manager, Maggie Russell. Maggie is very excited about Catrin being short listed, as are several other people in the department who have been very encouraging to Catrin as a writer.

They rightly see *Dune* being shortlisted as a return on their investment in Catrin, which is now being recognised by an Executive Producer of a network slot. Maggie takes the script down to London to show Pedr. On Thursday Catrin receives a call from Pedr saying he loves the script and I receive a call from Maggie asking how much we need and whether BBC Wales could show the film prior to its transmission on the network. I write to Jeremy Howe hoping that this news will take *Dune* off the shortlist and into the final selection. I copy the letter to Maggie Russell.

We hear nothing for a couple of weeks which does not mean we do nothing. We know that if we are selected all the questions will start and we want to be ready. This is the Catch 22 of pre-production. You have to be ready to go when the money is in place and have the best available team on hand in order to satisfy the executives that their money is safe – even on a tiny fiction film like *Dune*. This means knowing the availability of key personnel such as director of cinematography, designers, editors and, crucially, cast. I write to a good sound recordist in Wales and his wife, a make-up designer, and ask them if they will do the film for minimums, and if the sound recordist will throw in the equipment for a very low cost. I enclose the script hoping that they'll like it and say yes. I copy similar letters to other film technicians, actor's agents and musicians. We discuss music and opt for recorded pop music as we can clear under the blanket agreement for the BBC. I apply to the ACW Lottery Unit for the cost of two 35 mm prints of the film. If our application to the lottery for a cinema print is accepted we'll have to pay to clear the music for foreign television and theatre later.

We do all this whilst the kids are on holiday. I feel guilty drawing up budgets, writing lottery applications, location scouting (at least the kids get a day at the seaside), writing to casting agents. I arrange with a local child minder for Bryn to start in late September. I try not to worry about letting her down if the film is not selected. I try not to think about all the wasted hours and time away from the baby and my daughter during their summer holiday if the film is not selected. I try not to think about how little we are being paid even if the film is selected, given that we will have worked on it for months and that is not counting the time and creative energy that Catrin has invested writing the damn thing. I think bitter thoughts about people on salaries and not for the first time worry that this is the future – chasing tiny amounts of money and spending ridiculous amounts of time in the chase.

Catrin and I think about bigger films and wonder how possible they will be to make, given the demands of our families. We dream about making a feature film and hiring a big house with a nanny and the kids all mucking in together. I continue to breast feed Bryn every two hours day and night. Catrin tells me off every time I mention the primary school teacher option. We take it in turns to be focused and resolved but she is unrelenting in her desire to make the film. I am much more equivocal.

Monday September 14th: my partner is back at work full-time. I am working for Karl Francis, helping out writing development applications for Lottery and MEDIA 2 monies for feature film projects. My son Bryn is at home full-time and my daughter is back at school. I am trying to work either when Bryn is asleep or playing around my feet. He is curious about the keyboard on the Apple Mac and cries when I don't let him play. I feel that I should do paper work at night but I am too tired and anyway Bryn is up half the night as well. Bryn does a brilliant impersonation of me on the phone. His babble has perfect into-nation and he even manages to sound stressed. When I am not trying to type letters I am on the phone. At 6 p.m. I am giving the kids their tea and the phone rings again. I leave it to ring. Four hours later I ring my BT answering service to get the messages. At 6 p.m. Jeremy Howe had rung to say they definitely want to make *Dune*. I ring Catrin. We are both really thrilled. I ring Jeremy in the morning and he says they are in to the tune of £20,000. I ring Maggie Russell at BBC Wales and she is very pleased and says that they can probably find £15,000. I redo the budgets and settle on £41,000 – £24,000 from BBC Network and £17,000 from BBC Wales for the regional preview. This allows a small salary for Catrin and I of about £200 per week for the three month duration that the film will take to make, a contingency of £2,000, and a small production fee for Teliesyn which is both their due but also a standard conditional charge that any production company would make on an independent production wholly funded by a terrestrial broadcaster.

Maggie gives me an assurance over the phone that £17,000 is possible and asks me to submit the budget and the terms of the deal in writing so the paper work can go to Dai Smith, Head of English language Programmes at BBC Wales. A quiet bell of caution rings in my head. It is so quiet I hardly hear it – but for some reason I had not computed that Dai would have to give the final 'yes.' I imagined that the Head of Drama would be able to spend his drama budget as he saw fit without referring upwards. I have been spoilt by years of producing for Channel 4 in its early days when it was unheard of for a programme to be turned down once the commissioning unit had said they wanted it. As long as the contracts and budgets were agreed, no-one would really interfere with specialist editorial decision making.

I have to go to Sheffield for three days as I am an External Examiner at the Northern Media School. Whilst in Sheffield I receive a call from Maggie Russell saying Dai Smith is not inter-ested in *Dune*. Short films are very hard for regional broadcasters to schedule. My first response is fury. How could it take BBC

Wales so long to come to this negative decision? I am then furious with myself. To lose the film at this stage in the game can only be a failure of the producer. I should have left no stone unturned to try and find the matching money – sent the script to every possible financier in the business. I carry out my work as external examiner and catch the train down to Cardiff. At Bristol Station I stop and phone every one I can think of who is enthusiastic about the film to see if we can get Mr. Smith over his scheduling difficulties. I catch the wrong train and arrive in Weston-Super-Mare at 10 p.m., finally arriving wearily in Cardiff at midnight having set up meetings to try and reverse the decision for the following day.

An aside. In 1996 Richard Taylor wrote an article for *Vertigo* magazine outlining the various short film schemes that the British Regional Arts Associations have developed with local broadcasters. Wales was the only region in the whole of the UK that had no such scheme. At the time that the article was written I was working one day a week as production co-ordinator for the Wales Film Council. Mike Sweet, the then Chief Executive, and I had started negotiations with BBC Wales to try to establish such a scheme in Wales. I had been to the Edinburgh International Film Festival several times and seen the quite astonishing shorts emerging from Scotland under the Tartan Shorts scheme and also, whilst in Newcastle, seen a scheme established by Northern Arts and Tyne Tees Television. It seemed to me such an obviously good idea for broadcasters and regional production funds to join forces to produce work that would not otherwise be commissioned for television. In Scotland, the Oscars and other prestigious awards amassing in film-makers' offices and leading to a burgeoning feature film industry seemed to say it all. But in Wales the argument was not really won until Karl Francis was appointed as Head of Drama at BBC Wales. A film-maker himself and one who knew the independent film scene well and, having attended film festivals with his own work for years, was knowledgeable about the value of short films and the benefits they can have for broadcaster and film-maker alike. In Scotland, Tartan Shorts are produced by a producer/director/writer team but both BBC Wales and the Wales Film Council were cautious with this model and insisted that all four films be produced by one producer. I was nominated as the candidate, having spearheaded and campaigned for the scheme for several years. The four films (collectively entitled PICS: *The Confectioner* written and directed by Margaret Constantas; *Horse City* written and directed by Catrin Clarke; *Y* written and directed by Wyndham Price; and *Birdbrain* written by Greg Cullen and directed by Eric Styles) were completed in April 1997 and have gone on to win prizes and helped launch the film/television careers of all four writers and directors. The Wales Film Council then merged with its sister organisation to become Sgrîn and last year relaunched the shorts scheme as *Rarebits*, this time with four producer/director/writer teams. Thinking that the long hard argument for short films had been won, it came as a blow to hear that BBC Wales were continuing to have problems thinking of ways to schedule them.

Catrin and I attend several meetings that I have set up from Bristol railway station to try to persuade BBC Wales to invest in *Dune* as planned, and Jeremy Howe telephones Dai Smith. By the end of the day we have the desired result.

We start shooting the week of the worst floods in South Wales for nearly a century. The rain is spectacular. Our sound recordist's house is flooded and he asks me to find a replacement. We schedule all the fine weather scenes (the day on the sand dunes and the garden transformed into a dune landscape) for the beginning of the week so that we are ready to go when the sun shines. The sun does shine in ten minute blocks followed by torrential rain. The sky is full of spectacular rainbows. Film crews are resilient and everyone remains full of optimism and good humour. By Thursday we have to go to Merthyr Mawr to shoot the dune sequence as we have run out of days. Catrin's earlier film *Horse City* has been chosen for *The Talent* (a BBC network competition for the best short film shown on the BBC in the proceeding year) and the director of the show wants to shoot a location interview with Catrin. We choose the Merthyr Mawr location and I drive her in torrential rain through flooded roads to the sand dunes where we are supposed to be shooting Donna and her kids having a glorious day out in the sun.

Merthyr Mawr is a spectacular location covering several miles of some of the highest sand dunes in Wales. They are a challenge to climb, and kids from Cardiff and around toboggan down their steep slopes. The director of *The Talent* and I climb these slopes (her in black leather stiletto boots) to find the film crew huddled under large umbrellas trying to keep themselves and the film equipment dry.

They have shot about half of what we scheduled and are way past their lunch break. Between the breaks in the rain we shoot a difficult tracking shot and an important sequence for the narrative and then decide to call it a day. Most of what Catrin wanted to achieve has to be rethought and we come away with the bare bones of the narrative in the can. Everyone is hungry, wet and tired. The following day the sun shines for hours on end for the first time in a fortnight. We get the difficult "dune in the garden shot" no problem and wrap the film.

The editing process is reasonably problem free. Catrin's three children join us in the cutting room every day after school and are amazingly disciplined. They are old enough to know how important the process is and bring books and drawing materials with them, their pictures decorating the cutting room. Coyan, Catrin's middle child is in the film and he really enjoys seeing the process through. The major problem is that the film, including titles, cannot run for longer than 9 minutes and 15 seconds. We realise that the script as written is nearer 14 minutes. It is an inexact science timing the length of a screen play with the ball park estimate being one page to a minute. The continuity person had said the script was slightly long but the script editor had also timed it and thought it ran at about ten minutes. The solution is to cut out the entire sub plot concerning the gardening competition. We have to have the cut approved by both BBC Network and BBC Wales and this takes some organising. We have a few problems with the music and the dub but the film is completed by Christmas and everyone seems pleased.

In February we hear from the Arts Council of Wales Lottery Unit that they will pay for two 35mm prints of the film so it can be theatrically released and go to international festivals. They give us all the money I have applied for minus the wages element for Catrin and myself. Seeing a film through grading and dubbing, design of titles and clearing music for theatrical release is very time consuming. I am devastated by this decision. This is yet more work for absolutely no money. I am tempted to turn it down, deliver the film as a television film and forget the film festival and small theatrical shorts circuit. When the final cost reports are completed Catrin and I will have earned £1,000 each by making *Dune*. On a weekly basis this works out at less than £60 per week.

So why do it and what is the point of making short films? They are hard to schedule for some broadcasters and cinema exhibition is minimal. I am no rookie producer out to make a name for myself but a fairly hardened professional with twenty years' film and television experience behind me. At the cast and crew screening of *Dune* a BBC drama director says to me that he can see no point in making programmes that less than 10 million people are going to watch. Anything else is an indulgence and a waste of licence payers' money. I sit and argue with him for what seems like hours. I tell Catrin everything that he has said which plunges her into a deep depression.

Like the fairy that is not invited to the christening party, his curses cast a spell on the film. We are no longer pleased but embarrassed by our offspring and somehow we have to find a magic formula that will break his spell.

I find the answer in discovering, finally, what it is about the short film that I like. Short film has to throw away many of the common rules of the dramatic that obsess television culture. It has no time for intricate parallel story lines, it has no time for character development and therefore no time for back story. The vast majority of short films therefore have to forsake conventions that insist on the psychology and motivations of characters. If story-telling is about putting a man up a tree, throwing stones at him and then finding a way to get him out of the tree then the short film has no truck with why the man is in the tree in the first place. It is the antithesis of the soap opera or the drama serial. Its closest cousin is the feature film or the advertisement but it is also vastly different from them as well. When an art form is freed from the conventions of mainstream drama it becomes *per se* the site of experimentation, and that is what makes the short film format so exciting both for the producer and the viewer who is lucky enough to stumble across one in the television schedule or on those rare occasions in the cinema when they are programmed.

The short film will never be the mainstream of television nor can it ever be an 18 million viewer crowd pleaser. But despite this the *Video Nation* short which also dispenses with the conventions of plot and character development tells its audience a more simple and 'entertaining' truth than any six part docu-soap. Its brevity suits the amateur status of its originator, and its difference from the 'flow' of television output makes us watch it with a different set of expectations.

It is the marginality and innate experimental nature of short films that make them such a 'problem' for the BBC in Wales. For a broadcaster that has been repeatedly criticised for the amount of hours they manage to 'get' onto the network, BBC Wales has shown little confidence in promoting and lauding their commissioned home grown talent. For a few weeks in January, Jeremy Howe invited me to work in the 10x10 office in Bristol. The Talent had just been broadcast and the production staff were telling me how fiercely BBC Northern Ireland, BBC Scotland and BBC Films argue for their product to be part of this competition. In Wales there was no evidence that anyone thought it important or even knew. Catrin received no publicity and no acknowledgement that a film she had made with the BBC in Wales was being broadcast on the network as part of a national competition. In a recent study BBC Wales' contribution to BBC1 and BBC2 has grown from 21 hours to 43 hours over the last three years, yet only 19% of Network programmes from the National Regions come from Wales. BBC Wales' problem with short films is only a very small symptom of what is a much larger problem, but the success of *Tartan Shorts* in Scotland and *Northern Lights* in Northern Ireland should make broadcasters in Wales think differently about scheduling and promoting short films, and what they can do for an indigenous fiction, film and television industry. This is beginning to happen. Hopefully *Rarebits*, which is the successor to PICS, will become an established collaboration between BBC Wales and Sgrîn and Big Little Pictures, the new HTV Wales 24 minute short film scheme, is a definite step in the right direction. These films will need to be nurtured and publicised once they are made, scheduled and packaged with pride. They can provide both film-maker and audience with a site where experimentation can lead to innovation. They also provide a platform for the amateur, the dispossessed, the ambitious and the mad house wife to tell their stories.

Editor's Acknowledgements

I would like to acknowledge the generous help and support of a number of people during the production of this book. Firstly all the contributors who stuck with the project despite it taking a great deal of time to reach fruition: the film and tv companies who generously supplied stills and photographs, namely, S4C, HTV, BBC Wales, Metrodome, Universal Pictures and September Films: the friends, colleagues and students in Theatre and Media Drama at the University of Glamorgan who are always unfailingly supportive; the Regional Research Fund at Glamorgan that has provided a research award which led indirectly to this book being conceived; my patient contact at Seren, Mick Felton; my family, Mitch, Sam and Beth, and finally Julian Upton, who spent six months as a research assistant at Glamorgan and who was originally to have been my co-editor on this book if he had not gone on to greater things; he completed a lot of the preliminary research and I am sincerely grateful to him for his help and cheerful support.

Publisher's Acknowledgements

The stills in the plate section are published with the kind permission of the following: BBC Wales: *Food for Ravens, Streetlife, Trip Trap;* HTV Ltd: *In the Company of Strangers;* Metronome Distribution: *Human Traffic;* September Films: *House of America* (photographs by Mark Tillie); S4C: *Branwen, Canterbury Tales, Dafydd, Elenya, Gadael Lenin, Hedd Wyn, Pam fi Duw?, Un Nos Ola Leuad, Y Mapiwr.*

Index

Index